1. **The Book:** Cultivating A People for God **(CAPFG)** presents a fresh approach to spirituality and discipleship. It combines special inspirations with over 25 years of pastoral experience. It is specially written for pastors, seminary students, and serious church leaders.

2. **Translations:** The original English book has been **translated** into **7 other languages**. 1) *Bulgarian* & 2) *Swahili* are in print. The 3) *French, 4) Portuguese, 5) Urdu, 6) Hindi, 7) Marathi* translations are available in un-edited digital form.

3. **The CAPFG Mission** (Private mission) emerged during the pandemic in 2020. We offer the CAPFG course for the certificate, bachelor and masters level credits. We have seen over 500 pastors trained for the certificate level, 80 bachelor's (4) credits, and is engaging at least 1,500 high school students now in Tanzania, great results in India, Pakistan and Kenya – all through Zoom classes. We have documented many touching life transformation testimonies.

Recent CAPFG Newsletters: QR Codes

News 2022-11

News 2023-03

News 2023-07

4. **Discipleship Multiplication Program:** The **CAPFG** approach is effective in both ***transient (high-people-flow) environment*** as well as ***stable city churches***. It is usable in ***small church*** as well as ***mega churches***. It contains *minimal cultural baggage,* and proved very effective for the mission fields.

Enoch Kwan

34 Dewberry Drive, Markham
Ontario   L3S 2S1
enkwan@gmail.com 416-877-6287

Cultivating a People for God

A Gift from Enoch Kwan

enkwan@gmail.com
1-416-877-6287
Comments & Donations welcome

Enoch Kwan

WESTBOW
PRESS®
A DIVISION OF THOMAS NELSON
& ZONDERVAN

This book is a work of non-fiction. Unless otherwise noted, the author
and the publisher make no explicit guarantees as to the accuracy of
the information contained in this book and in some cases, names of
people and places have been altered to protect their privacy.

WestBow Press books may be ordered through booksellers or by contacting:

WestBow Press
A Division of Thomas Nelson & Zondervan
1663 Liberty Drive
Bloomington, IN 47403
www.westbowpress.com
1 (866) 928-1240

Because of the dynamic nature of the Internet, any web addresses or
links contained in this book may have changed since publication and
may no longer be valid. The views expressed in this work are solely those
of the author and do not necessarily reflect the views of the publisher,
and the publisher hereby disclaims any responsibility for them.

Any people depicted in stock imagery provided by Getty Images are
models, and such images are being used for illustrative purposes only.
Certain stock imagery © Getty Images.

Interior Image Credit: Enoch Kwan

Scriptures taken from the Holy Bible, New International Version®, NIV®.
Copyright © 1973, 1978, 1984, 2011 by Biblica, Inc.™ Used by permission
of Zondervan. All rights reserved worldwide. www.zondervan.com The
"NIV" and "New International Version" are trademarks registered in
the United States Patent and Trademark Office by Biblica, Inc.™

ISBN: 978-1-9736-5457-5 (sc)
ISBN: 978-1-9736-5458-2 (dj)
ISBN: 978-1-9736-6887-9 (cb)
ISBN: 978-1-9736-5456-8 (e)

Library of Congress Control Number: 2019902742

Printed in the United States of America.

WestBow Press rev. date: 7/8/2019

I thank You, Lord, for the twenty-five years' journey of writing this book and for what You have taught me, which I am still learning! May this book be a blessing to our generation according to Your will.

I pray that you would be as excited and attentive to God
when reading it as when I was receiving and writing it.
. . .
as there is no value for me to spend 24 years to
write a book that convey only an old message - that
other able authors have already written.
. . .
I have no right to waste your time reading something you have
already known, or wasting your money to buy such a book!
. . .
You may need to resist the temptation of complacency with your
current situation and more importantly with your paradigm.

Happy prayerful reading!
To God be the glory.

CONTENTS

PREFACE

This book is meant to help you to think and see things more from God's eternal perspective. It will try to draw your attention to God's yearning throughout the course of human history. That is not easy because we are comfortable with our temporal perspectives and like to keep everything under our control based on what we have learned in our time and culture.

I wrote this book primarily to call Christ's church to pay attention to and live according to what God wanted in the beginning and wants in the end. However, you will find it helpful in solving some of the problems you face with your ministry and your personal walk with God. Yet this helpfulness is only a by-product, because your problems are only overrun and melted away when you are blessed with God's presence as you first sought His heart and kingdom and accomplishing His plan.

This book clarifies the church's mission in a fresh perspective based on God's will for His people. It explores His simple requirements and instructions for Christians to live and engage easily to cultivate people for Himself. In the process of our journey together, you may find a new theological emphasis on God's original design of humanity and find new, deeper theological insights in the area of worship, stewardship, fellowship, discipleship. This may in fact challenge some of your church ministry approaches and spirituality paradigms.

We celebrate with the many regularly fruitful churches and Christians. They thrive in a time when the Christian faith is under attack. Unfortunately, many Christians and churches of all sizes around the world are experiencing crises in their spiritual journeys and in church ministries. No matter if you or your church is doing well or poorly, this book will still benefit you in many ways. Though my target readers are pastors and church leaders, any serious Christian can experience a rich spiritual journey reading it. If you believe in creation, the final judgment, and heaven,[1] you will find this book beneficial.

This book was written over twenty-seven years. Chapter 7, on assembled worship, was written earliest in 1991. It was a first-year seminary assignment. I made only minor adjustments in 2018. Chapters 4 and 11 came right out of my Doctor of Ministry degree work – a final focus paper[2], largely as they were written in 2008, and therefore contain the most external references just like any academic paper. My desire to write the book began in 1994 but the theological framework and title for the book was not settled until 2017 - after the Lord taught me as much as I could absorb in the process. I pray God will call on someone who sees the value in this message to continue the journey I traveled.

In the beginning, I wished God had asked a more able person to convey this message. Since I was prompted to write this book, I have been watching, searching, and hoping to see that someone else was called and had already written this message. I researched that in the doctoral program at Fuller Theological Seminary in 2000. In the end, I was convinced with fear and trembling, but also with joy in submission, for the calling to this mission. This mission is to bring to our generation an important message with a new theological perspective. I hope you will notice the broad and strong rooting in Scripture fresh and interesting. I pray you are as excited and attentive to God when reading it as I was when writing it.

If you want to receive the full benefit of this book, you may need to set aside some quiet time in a setting where you can converse with God while you interact with my thoughts. It will help tremendously if you have a readiness to say, "Lord, I am willing" as frequently as He appeals to you in the process. You may need to resist the temptation of complacency with your current situation and more importantly your paradigm. I hope you can see beyond the desired immediate results and turn your attention to God's eternal purpose, keeping the end—eternity—in mind.

I hope we share the desire to offer God, through our journeys together, a blessed people who choose to live their earthly lives by His will so that He will have now as well as in eternity what He wanted from the beginning. May the Holy Spirit speak His own message to

---

[1] This may include all religions that believe in one God—Protestantism, Roman Catholicism, Judaism, and even Islam.

[2] My doctor of ministry final focus paper was published by VDM Verlag on October 23, 2009, under the title *Towards a 4-ships Driven Culture*.

you as you journey through the text. I pray that your love for God our Father will grow as we fellowship through these pages. I hope God gets what He wants in and through you at the end of our journey together through your prayerful reading. I am confident you will not regret allowing this book to jump the long queue in your reading list.

I am not a good writer even in Chinese, my native language, and now I need to write in English! Please bear with my poor writing if you come across hard to read segments throughout this book. We must thank the editors including my wife too because they have worked very hard to bring the book to this level of readability. Sometimes, I wish God had not assigned me this difficult task. However, I gladly and thankfully took up the challenge because of my submission to Him. I pray that your journey through this book will stimulate in you a fresh love for God and that He will show you His plan for you, your family, your church, and the world.

Journeying through This Book

My family can attest that I made a pledge to write this book in 1994 as a new year's resolution - one year after I had received the insight. God, however, was not finished with me, and even now, more than two decades later, I am still learning it. My family and all others who know me enough can also attest to how the Four Ships concept has led me through a few trying and life-threatening circumstances, and how that has helped numerous people understand life according to God's will. With the benefits of such grace from God, my heart burns with the desire to share this with you to the point that I resigned from my heavy pastoral role to focus on writing, and only doing light consulting duties among church leaders as time allows. I heartily invite you to join me through the journey of this book. I hope God will teach you directly and quickly the things He has taken so long to teach me.

This book will paint for you a vision of a renewed culture. The beginning chapters will help us to establish the framework for our study. They will help you to gradually think more in terms of God's own concerns, help you to be aware of your own cultural straitjacket. These chapters will stimulate you so that good reflective questions may be raised in your own heart.

Chapters 5 through 10 will help redefine and clarify the terms worship, stewardship, fellowship, and discipleship in a wider context. I have included chapter 11 to cover the relationship this Four Ships culture has with some other popular contemporary movements and how its theological framework may strengthen certain aspects to supplement those movements.

In these chapters and the appendices, I will share with you the exciting possibilities of building a culture that pleases God, and how this new culture will bring value and meaning to ministry, life at work, at home, and even in politics. I hope you find God speaking to you in a unique way so you will own His will, because of and even despite of what you read in this book.

INTRODUCTION

In God's Mind and Heart

Keeping the End in Mind

You and I have a beginning and will likely have an end in a time line on earth. We experience faith and church in a time line also, having a beginning and possibly an end if the Lord tarries. If you were like me at one point, you may also be so busy with the ministries and church activities that you only have the time and energy to deal only with the present and the near future. Few of us have the habit of thinking in terms of years and decades ahead let alone in terms of eternity.

When we as church leaders think only in short-term, we can get bogged down with business without the ability to reflect on the direction and destination we should be going. Our ministries and those we suppose to lead and bless would likely missing out God's blessings without notice. When we serve only the immediate businesses and ministries, we might even be serving not God but something else without knowing it for years. In 2000, Eddie Gibbs wrote about the situation of the North American mainline denominations.

> Those who have turned to Christianity and churches seeking truth and meaning have left empty-handed, confused by the apparent inabilities themselves to implement the principles they professed. Churches, for the most part, have failed to address the nagging anxieties and deep-seated fears of the people, focusing

xv

instead upon outdated or secondary issues and proposing tired or trite solutions.[3]

I think this is still happening. Many seekers left empty-handed after a short journey with us in our churches, and we are also losing our second generation and longtime churchgoers because of various reasons not yet identified. On top of the institutional decline and human disappointments is a more serious consequence: God's disappointment in the churches and His children. God will question His people on judgment day for these things.

However, we should be glad to know that it was not always this bad. We saw at one point in history that Christians were giving great testimony and bringing many to Christ. The society was turned totally upside down as the Great Revival came in the 1800's. Then time changed again. As His church and His children today, some of us may not be giving Him all He longs for—people living according to His will and bringing disciples for Christ! What happens here in our segment of the time line affects many people's lives and above all, it affects how God feels.

God does not live in a time line as we do; He transcends time. The beginning and the end of time are transparent to Him. His decision of creating us in His image and wanting to share love with us does not change. God's will for us to live in the way He planned will not change either. Though we have sinned and are doomed to die because of our wrong choices, in the end, God's plan will prevail; He will have a perfect people He created and saved by His perfect will and some of us will be a part of it.

Let My People Live!

It all began in the beginning: God created and loved humanity. That does not change despite our sin and being cut off from Him. Even before the beginning, an idea spilled out from His infinite riches: What God wanted began with His own eternal, abundant, overflowing love. He desired to create a special new kind of being. God planned for them to function beautifully, holy and reflect Him on their earthly journeys, and more importantly to be in love with Him forever. So He prepared the environment by creating time, space, and the physical and spiritual

---

[3] Gibbs, *ChurchNext*, 16.

realms. At the proper time, God created the physical human form, and with the breath of His Spirit, humanity received the most precious gift—a portion of God's nature. Adam and Eve were like God having a spirit, and were intelligent, passionate, able to communicate in speech and were granted freedom of choice and other characteristics like God. He placed Adam and Eve in the garden He had prepared. He saw that everything was very good indeed. The beautiful scene shone with the perfection of His handiwork and holiness. With His will and blessing, Adam and Eve and the whole of humanity after should live forever with Him.

Yet something happened one fateful day. The devil worked through a snake to make Eve and then Adam tragically stumble. According to God's prehistoric rules, they would have been doomed to die that day they ate the fruit from the forbidden tree. Since then, humankind has been a captive of the devil. God's crowning creation that was meant for love has been snatched from His loving side. Humankind lost the blessings and God lost His beloved people.

Though new children could be born after the fall, eternal life was denied for them. All human would ultimately face death, hopelessness and meaninglessness. This is a dark tragedy on earth and in heaven. Ever since then God and humankind were seeking each other. The humankind's search for meaning, satisfaction, and direction through the past centuries apart from God has come to nothing. Tears and hopelessness in the wandering converted many souls to some man-made religions, and others to substance abuse and wild lifestyles. There are so many tears on earth as humankind yearns for answers in human ways without seeing the true light in their wandering. Our humanistic yearning and searching keep yielding only emptiness because of our departure from God. Too many people did not know that only God can really be the answer to our emptiness because He is the only one who defined the meaning of humankind. Humankind laments over our being lost and are desperate for we had indeed lost so much since that day.

Yet, though by God's grace some of us learned through God's revelations in the Bible the need to reconcile with God and are also taught to be good Christians. However, most of everything we learn is selfishly about our own benefits, obligations, and thoughts. I wonder how many of us have ever given thought or heart to notice what that tragedy meant to God. How does God, who started the goodness of it all, feel then and now because His masterpiece of creation that bears

His image is broken? Do we even care to find out and understand God's loss and the pain He suffered in that process?

God suffered a loss that was so enormous beyond human words can fully describe. God had decided to sacrifice His Son to restore the situation. My heart sank when I caught a glimpse of what God had lost that day. When He lost Adam and Eve to sin, it was like losing His very only Son! Tears swell in my eyes as I type these words understanding how much we meant to God. God has been in tears since that day. He yearned for a restoration with His bride. It was illustrated once in Exodus: the Israelites were crying, and God heard their pleas. Through Moses, He spoke to Pharaoh and demanded he let His people go. God has already a salvation plan. He demands that His people be released from the bondage of sin and be returned to His loving side.

The Son of God became flesh and lived with us for a while; He preached with authority and revealed the truth like no one ever had revealed before. He demonstrated the Father's approval and glory by miracles, teaching, confrontation with false religion, and eventually through His innocent death and glorious resurrection. The Lord Jesus called twelve disciples to be helpers and close witnesses. He led them every step of the way. He gave them authority and a mission. Though our Lord had the power to live forever on earth to preach and convert the world, He departed and gave a commission to the twelve and other followers. He entrusted His disciples with the work of freeing His people, whom we now call the church. The Church's mission is to help free people from the bondage of the devil through the Gospel, and through Christian discipleship to offer to God the kind of people He meant to have in the beginning. These people should, by His will and instructions, function beautifully once again on their earthly journeys, holy and have a loving relationship with God in their daily faith and lives.

God wants His people back! God wants His people to live again! Our heavenly Father yearned so much for His people that He had already sacrificed a part of Himself - His Only Son to gain us back. As He once said: "Let My people go!" He has likewise such a strong yearning in His heart. God the almighty pronounced in a loud voice that resounded through heaven and earth as He sent His Son. Let My people live! I pray that you have heard His call in your heart too and joined Him in His endeavor to bring His people back.

In fact, churches around the world have tried their best to fulfill this commission. However, humankind changes easily. Sometimes, churches are focused well on the objective, but other times, on other secondary things like methods and processes. In so many cases I have seen that programs, methods and institutional elements have become so prominent and drawing most of the attention and church leaders forget why we exist as Christ's Church. Indeed, churches have explored and placed emphasis on such a variety of theologies and practices that religious life has become very complicated and heavily burdening both pastors and congregations around the world. God's People are now carrying a gigantic burden psychologically and spiritually. The weight and stresses the old Chosen People experienced under oppression in Egypt may be a good illustration for our situation! For years, I have searched for answers to this question: How can I become a God pleasing person? I believe God does not require a complex, sophisticated, Western, postmodernist education for people to understand His will. I want an answer simple enough that a child or anyone who may have only a few years of education could understand it and live in the same way I can.

This book is an invitation for you to look at a very simple answer God had revealed to me in this over two decades.

Please share with me too your findings regarding this question.

Let us begin.

CHAPTER 1

A Simple, Life-Transforming Way Exists

Simple Life-Transforming Conversations

First, a few real-life stories—cultivating people for God everywhere.

June 2017—Coffee Shop at Skopje's Ancient City Center, Macedonia

I was having a drink at a coffee shop with a Macedonian pastor, his wife, and their daughter, who is also their ministry partner. After listening to the pastor's heart for his ministry and the challenges he faced, I shared with them the concept of cultivating a people for God in God's way with what I call the four "ships"—worship, stewardship, fellowship, and discipleship.

The pastor and his wife immediately caught the value of the simple concept. They were so sure that the message would make a significant impact on their network of churches that they invited me to speak on that topic in their pastoral leadership conference the next year. But another conference came just four months after and I could share it there. I went the next year too. To God's glory, pastors and church leaders were blessed with an encounter with God and spiritual fellowship with each other when we shared the message.

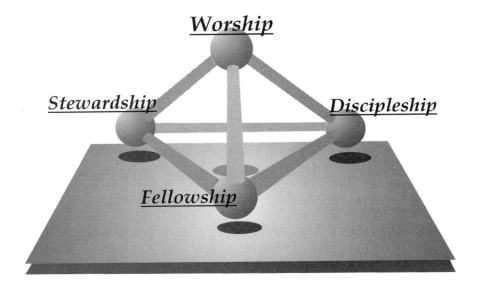

June 2018—A Group Dinner

Pastor M was acting as my interpreter for his mentor Pastor E and his son David. As I shared my objective and priority of discipleship, Pastor M was caught by his sudden understanding of God's heart and forgot to interpret. He paused to thank and praise God before he could go on to translate my sentences.

The next day, Pastor M reported to us that Pastor E and David were no longer the same people. "They cannot go back to their old selves," he said. Pastor M promised to translate this book into Bulgarian with a close spiritual friend. David also recognized the value, and they are planning to ask me to speak with their youth leaders.

October 2011—Thirty-Six Thousand Feet over Canada

The woman on my right was awake in the middle of the fifteen-hour flight. I prayed for an opportunity to share the gospel with her or at least some encouraging words. By God's grace, an intentional spiritual conversation followed. As we talked, I scribbled pictorial notes on the back of my boarding pass. About an hour later, this highly educated woman who had never heard the crux of the gospel in her Communist background realized the ultimate authority of God over her life. She also expressed willingness to welcome God's invitation to salvation through Jesus Christ. I gladly obliged when she asked if she could keep the notes I had drawn during our conversation.

November 2014—Vancouver

My nephew Michael engaged attentively in a serious conversation with me in his family's living room. My brother and sister-in-law came home one after the other and passed by silently with smiles. Michael was set to graduate from university in two years. I was concerned about him because I had heard concerned comments about the church he was attending. I decided to share the Four Ships concept with him to see if it would help him find clear spiritual direction. After some chitchat, I asked his permission to present my insights. His parents were delighted to see the light in his eyes afterward.

The following day, his mother asked me to speak to Michael's younger sister, and Margaret's response was just as enthusiastic as Michael's had been at the life-transforming insight.

August 2011— Toronto in A Couple's Living Room

An East Asian Christian couple had asked me to counsel them. The tension was taut and threatening from the start. The husband and wife would not stop accusing each other in strong, mean words. Neither of them answered any charge accused of, let alone admitted any fault. The shouting match allowed very little space for me to speak.

Eventually, I explained to them the Four Ships concept showing them the supporting scriptures. With the notes I scribbled along the way, the couple saw right away their overbearing attitude that had overtaken God's authority in their relationship as well as their personal behavior. They realized that their faulty worship of God had rippled through their entire lives and had prevented them from building a God-centered family. They saw how their careless individualism had suffocated the sweet fellowship they were supposed to build and enjoy as husband and wife. Their degenerated relationship had also robbed them of the opportunity to lead their children to follow Christ correctly.

Their relationship problem was not solved that day, but they gained a spiritual framework that helped them filter and examine what they needed to do with each other.

2006—Under a Tree at our house

I was speaking with Andrew, my son's best friend. My conversation with this university student turned into a fellowship on spiritual matters. I described the Four Ships concept to him, and his reception of it was very positive. He admitted right away that his spiritual life would no longer be the same because of this insight.

It was a joy to see him grow spiritually as a young man and my son enjoy having such a good friend. Up to 2017, Andrew and my son served in a similar capacity of leading a youth group in different churches. They meet regularly for exercise and fellowship.

2012—Hong Kong

As I was writing this chapter in Hong Kong in 2012, I received a call from Pastor William, whom I had met two days earlier. We had had at most ten minutes of interaction at the end of my visit to his church the previous Sunday. I had shared the Four Ships concept with him, and he had immediately shown interest in it.

Among Pastors

Since 1993, I have conversed with many pastors and church leaders who poured out their concerns for their ministries. I discovered that issues such as traditionalism, church-growth, ministry survival, institutionalism, Phariseeism, power struggles, loss of direction, lack of spiritual vitality, ineffective programming, incompetent staff, secularism, commercialism, and many other problems were more common than I had imagined. These have been perpetual concerns that form identifiable hindering subcultures in the churches. As opportunities allowed, I depicted the life-transforming Four Ships concept by word or pen on any writable surface including table napkins and scrap paper, and most people found it helpful and agreed that it aligned with God's heart.

I have lost count of how many times I have shared the Four Ships concept. Except on rare occasions, even among people of diverse backgrounds, people have immediately understood and seen the validity and value of these principles. The Four Ships principles are based on God's revelation rooted deep and widespread scriptures throughout the Bible.

Human Nature—Dynamic by Design

The Four Ships concept is not yet widely known or practiced, but it can be readily discovered through simple Bible study. Since 1993, God has been soaking me with thoughts about the idea and has shown me its meanings in scripture. I am convinced it is of God because of clear evidence in the Bible and God's multiple illuminations while I was in fellowship with Him—and sometimes from His own initiation. If it is from God, it must be good, and it must work. I became so convinced of this that I use it as a foundational concept for my personal life as well as for ministry.

Pastor Edward, whom I am supervising as our church plant pastor, heard the concept for the first time in September 2009. He commented in early 2012, "I accepted it before because you shared it with me then, but only recently have I discovered just how important and powerful the concept is. You should really share it with our fellow pastors."

Pastor Edward has acquired a new spiritual map that helps bring himself and his congregation far beyond his charismatic tradition. Healing, filling with the Holy Spirit, and speaking in tongues now have proper slots in this richer spiritual framework.

As I had with Pastor Edward, I have often asked other pastors, "What in your own spiritual life is so worthwhile and God-approved that you would duplicate it in the people Christ has entrusted to you?" My own answer to this was, "I would duplicate my heart and spirit in worship, stewardship, fellowship, and discipleship." It integrates my walk with God to fulfill His mission as I enjoy the life He designed for me. This heart and spirit help me endure the pains, sorrows, and challenges that come with life and ministry. The Four Ships concept opens our hearts and lives to be channels for God to cultivate people for Himself.

Can a Simple Cure-All Exist?

Since April 2012, I have visited many churches and spoke with Christians and non-Christians to study this concept. I am convinced that tradition-bound, self-centered, human-centered religionism and churchism are the central problems in our church subcultures today.

Does a simple cure-all exist in the face of these problems? No one on earth is qualified to answer that. However, I have set down certain assumptions in the course of my faith pilgrimage. First, I believe my mother who had less than a third-grade education can be a good, productive Christian because the world is filled with common people like her. She knows only Cantonese and a limited number of Chinese words and has no possibility of learning Greek or Hebrew. She has no training to help her deliver a sermon or teach a Sunday school class. The common people around the world are just like her. If God demands any more abilities or achievements, most people would be hopeless in becoming "good" Christians. Thus I believe there must be that simple thing that even a child can follow to become a God-pleasing, mission-effective, life-enjoying, godly person. Of course, my simple assumption is useless unless God agrees with it.

In 1993, God started revealing His plan to me during a sermon preparation on a mission trip. This is not a special insight I could claim as my own because of my scriptural knowledge or Bible-interpretation skills. It is not something God has allowed only me to see. It is rather something that can be explained very simply and rests on a wide base of crucial passages in the Bible. Religious people throughout history who believe in simplicity have also been in search for a simple, overarching principle. God will give us the grace to understand it when we are ready for it. It is in the passage in which Jesus spoke to the Pharisees in Matthew 22:34–40. As for me, once I saw it, I started to gradually free myself of the cultural straitjacket that binds me and many well-meaning people. We have all been slaves to traditions, human-centeredness, self-centeredness, and a religionist mind-set. I am still learning new, exciting things in this freedom journey and I feel the freedom daily.

CHAPTER 2

God's People—Now and Then

If we are to assess how well any company or community is doing, we must first understand its purpose and specifications. Humankind did not come into existence by our own will or purpose, nor did God's chosen people choose themselves for any purpose of their own. God created us in His image to be His people and from His own initiative He redeemed us by His Son. Both creation and redemption are of God and for His purposes.

God intended Adam, Eve, and their offspring to be His pleasing companions, to appreciate Him, and to fellowship with Him and each other. He designed them to live in a sin-free state to manage the earth. He was disappointed when Eve and Adam fell at the temptation of the devil. However, He intended to save human beings, give them the opportunity to be holy again, and call them to a holy mission. A mission of restoring what He deemed the original goodness in creation. In evaluating the performance of this mission, the language used should reflect the original purposes and values of God's creation and His mission of restoring people to Himself. As we go into making observations and assess performance, take note of the words and the deep value systems they represent in the various descriptions. You will discover some difficulties God's people have faced in history and get a grasp on the spiritual issues the church as God's people faces today.

A Very Large Church

In 2002, I attended a very large church in southern California with over forty-five thousand worshippers. The church was obviously purpose driven with very active ministries for all ages. The physical facilities were amazing and impressive. The service was smooth and led by very capable people, great singers, and a loud band. The congregation of over four thousand per seating seemed to follow the program well; the sermon, the scripture reading, and the greetings were all well done. The atmosphere was down to earth in an earth-community connection sense. It was very compassionate and friendly. However, one thing I found lacking in its active and rich Sunday service program was my usual connection with God, a sense of intimately upward yet community-united worship.

After the service, I had to spend private time in prayer to worship God to compensate for the feelings of being left out by the congregation and God alike. My experience at that church service may have been distorted because I visited only once. However, because of this church's seeming success, it is admired by many leaders and pastors (including me) of similar and smaller churches around the world. We may cheer and celebrate the success in overall ministry, numbers, and vibrant activities. Yet true, deep-hearted celebration may not be a common experience among congregants in such worship services.

Why do so many follow the model of that church? The fact that churches around the world strive to emulate the success formula of this church (and achieve various degrees of success) points out one thing: churches that look to that one for a blueprint or formula for success are at a loss. They are out looking for a method that will improve their current state of being a church. Something is missing from these learning churches, and they consider being purpose-driven a good, reasonable and attractive solution.

Some questions should be asked, however. What do these learning churches feel missing that led them to seek a new model? What is *it*?[4] What part of their own current way do they believe does not please God? Will this successful church give them the ultimate answer? What does this purpose-driven church really doing to please God and follow His plan that you see that you want to follow? Would it be that they are trying to do church in a way they thought was fine yet in fact be missing God's will in some way?

A Medium-Size Church

After studying statistics other writers have reported, I wanted to experience as many churches as possible. I sought a church that had a

---

[4] Craig Groeschel's book *It* grasps just what is missing.

track record of growing through evangelism. While traveling in Hong Kong, I found on the internet a church I thought fit this description and attended a service there. I was so blessed by the simple service that I stayed for the next service. Both were very simple gatherings of about eighty people each and were held in the same hundred-seat room. The leaders were humble and demonstrated their respect for God and obedience to His teaching and mission.

The songs were not loud. The singers were not impressive, and the pianist was stumbling along obviously lacking in skill, practice, and confidence. Yet the atmosphere demonstrated through the prayers, announcements, and sermons showed humble respect for God. I felt God was there accepting their humble worship and would bring fruit to their efforts of disciple making. Incidentally, this church did not closely adhere to the five purposes many churches learned from the very large church mentioned in the preceding section. I felt that the church was on a spiritual journey in Christ and dear to God's heart.

Another Very Large Church

A seminary professor who was teaching a class on church leadership and management was asked to describe the spirituality of his church of over twenty-five thousand members. He paused for quite a while before telling us that they worshipped, sang all kinds of songs, and prayed on various occasions. His answer suggested that praying and attending worship were the major spiritual things they did. The class was quite in awe of the professor's lack of clarity in his answer. While he could teach doctoral students the principles of leading and managing large churches, there was a real possibility that the huge church he attended was at a loss concerning clarifying its spiritual direction and essence.

Could it have been that the main concern of the pastor, who was leading over twenty-five thousand souls, was the smooth operation and expansion of the institution that bears the name of Christ; rather than calling and cultivating people to a spiritual walk with God in the name of Christ?

Medium-Size Churches

During the last ten years, I have had numerous opportunities to speak with pastors and leaders of many small and medium-size churches (one hundred to eight hundred worshippers). My question has always been how well they thought their churches pleased God especially in terms of making and multiplying disciples for Jesus. In most cases, leaders and pastors had to switch from the mind-set of institutional operation or program execution to follow the direction of our conversation—on how well their churches were pleasing God.

I found that most pastors and church leaders were primarily concerned with developing programs and achieving tasks or projects in the context of their ministry challenges including growth, decline, building upgrades, financial issues, power struggles, and a shortage of functional leadership. My deeper involvement as a consultant to some churches further revealed one key issue pastors often mentioned: the lack of love for God and the lack of direction in discipleship.

I had also found myself being task driven in my role as pastor of a small congregation that was turning around. I was the only paid staff and was without even a secretary. Leading a small congregation demands more of the pastors' time as he has fewer talented people with which to share his workload. Pastors of small churches easily get burned out as they look at their peers in more-established churches who are enjoying success. In many small churches, the pressure of preparing and delivering weekly sermons is not relieved due to the lack of other staff and funds for inviting outside speakers. Mundane tasks compete for energy that would otherwise be devoted to making and multiplying disciples according to Jesus's command (Matthew 28:19–20).

In large and small churches, many institutional and program concerns compete for attention and leave few resources for deeper, quieter things such as monitoring the spiritual state of things and waiting to hear God's direction. Fellowship with God and His Spirit can become a precious but rare experience.

Analysis of Difficulties across Time

However drastic or terrible this may seem, this phenomenon is not new. What I described here reflects exactly what happened to God's chosen people in the Old Testament. This issue was also addressed in prophetic messages and even the book of Revelation. Busyness then and now caused things to become shallow and take on the form but not the essence of holiness. Leaders and people alike lose their first love for God and disrespect God while gathering in His name.[5] As He

---

[5] The book of Malachi.

did in the days of Malachi, the Lord is calling us to repent our spiritual corruption.

In 2000, Eddie Gibbs wrote about the situation of North American mainline denominations. I quote again:

> Those who have turned to Christianity and churches seeking truth and meaning have left empty-handed, confused by the apparent inabilities themselves to implement the principles they professed. Churches, for the most part, have failed to address the nagging anxieties and deep-seated fears of the people, focusing instead upon outdated or secondary issues and proposing tired or trite solutions.[6]

In the last few decades, at least these three big church growth movements (no particular order) have had a certain level of success in reviving the churches around the world. The first is Pastor Rick Warren's purpose-driven movement. It has been a great phenomenon embraced by many churches across the globe. It focuses on purposefulness in church ministry and personal spiritual life as well. Second, Pastor Bill Hybels's Global Leadership Summit drew more and more people to focus on cultivating high-quality Christian leaders for the churches and the marketplace. Third, the natural church development (NCD) approach introduced and promoted by Christian Schwarz on the other hand has been helping the more church-oriented paths. Small groups, worship, and music renewal has been continuing since the 1980s. The house church movement, satellite churches, and organic churches are also bandwagons that promote some better ways of being and doing church.

Two thousand years of doctrinal debates and establishments, church governance developments, and reformations have not solved the problem. Revivals and waves of renewal rose and dwindled, and we could only dream of their recurrence. It is only a dream to think that any people or the ministries they operate would stay successful once they applied this method. No one has ever invented or seen a perfect program that guarantee spiritual success. No one has yet identified such state of arrival or completion in personal or corporate spiritual journeys. We all fall short of God's standard because we are human.

---

[6] Gibbs, *ChurchNext*, 16.

God designed us to be on a constant journey of choosing to do His will by our God-given free choice. Because of this free choice and our inherent sinful nature, our choices are never perfect especially after Adam and Eve's fall.

I intentionally visited many churches to find out how well congregations connected with God and His commission. Out of the dozens of churches I visited, only a few demonstrated a real relationship with God while the rest to me were no more than religious gatherings with little spiritual essence. I am alarmed at how poorly God's people are doing in fulfilling their call to be His people and fulfill His mission.

The chief problem of the chosen people in the Old Testament and even now is unfaithfulness to God and His commands. That causes problems in interpersonal relationships including injustice and mercilessness. While the temple worship in the Old Testament and Sunday services today are maintained alike, the essential relationship the chosen people had with God may have dried up today just as they did in the times of the prophets.

God spoke through the prophets once, and I am not surprised that He has the same comment about some of our churches today not because of their size but because of their lack of authenticity in their relationship with God.

> "Oh, that one of you would shut the temple doors, so that you would not light useless fires on my altar! I am not pleased with you," says the LORD Almighty, "and I will accept no offering from your hands. (Malachi 1:10)

> A modernized interpretation of the above Scripture may look like: Oh, that one of you would shut the *church* doors, so that you would not *gather falsely in my name*! I am not pleased with you, … and I will accept no *worship from your self-pleasing services.*

The threat of God's wrath was evident not only in the Old Testament. In Revelation, Jesus commanded the apostle John to write to the seven churches concerning their strengths and deficiencies. Christ approved of the seven churches' faithfulness to His name and teachings, their endurance through suffering, and their faithfulness in service. But He also denounced their excessive self-confidence, self-sufficiency, refusal to obey His teachings, and false repentance. He pointed out that the churches' lack of fervent love made them revolting to Him; they were like lukewarm water in His mouth.

He addressed the churches' acceptance of false teaching that had seeped into His church and caused a lack of awareness of truth and blatant sins among them (Revelation 2–3). What can we do to be found faithful and true rather than failing His call for us to be His people?

Why Don't We Ask Jesus?

The above question was not new either. Some men in Jesus's time had the right idea despite how Jesus admonished and even denounced them many times. The Pharisees was this religious sect Jesus denounced, but they were not so bad originally. They started as serious, religious people who grew dissatisfied with the lack of love and respect for God among the priests and the loose religious practice of their time. Despite their limited authority and resources, they found a way to keep their commitment to God by seriously studying the scriptures available to them.

In today's terms, they would be like movements that draw us back to study the Bible including Bible schools, Bible study, exegetical preaching, theological research, the study of biblical languages, starting seminaries, and many more. The Pharisees' writings during and before Jesus's time represents a rich tradition and a noble journey no less productive than ours; they produced volumes of commentaries and insights based on the scriptures.

The Sadducees during Jesus's time were more like the institutional tradition of the religious offices in the high church today. Pharisees and Sadducees fondly embraced their strength and particular theologies, and thus impossible to reconcile their theological differences. So, from their rich traditions, they approached Jesus. I am sure the incident was recorded not only to inform us today but was also intended prophetically to give people of all times directions on how to be God's people.

In Matthew 22:34–40, the Pharisees asked Jesus, "Teacher, which is the greatest commandment in the Law?" Today, that might sound like, "Lord Jesus, which of today's theologies and movements represent authentic Christian faith that God demands?" The intense debates between the religious sects of the day indicate that this question was not easy to answer. Out of genuine interest and humbleness or due to cunning scheming, the Pharisees threw that question at Jesus. I wonder if we are too proud or complacent today and thus do not feel the need to come to the Lord humbly to ask Him the same important question.

There is no value in asking such a question if one or more of the proposed solutions we see in the global Christian community are working perfectly. As I examined the leading solutions—a purpose-driven, seeker-friendly, leadership-essential, and natural church development—I found that they work only to an extent and fail to clearly connect the Christian daily walk and God's will. They are more churchy, too down to earth, and not close enough to God than I desire. I have been seeking a spirituality approach that dwells on salvation, church life, and church growth and a fully integrated framework of daily life. This framework must help me see the comprehensive interpretation and meaning of everything in life according to God's creative plan, redemption, discipleship, and life in eternity.

As I read Matthew 22:34 during my seminary days, I was caught by God's invitation to consider this question. I appreciate the Lord's leading to answer this question for me. Joy has overcome me too many times to count as I see God's foreknowledge despite human weaknesses, and His grace revealed His all-encompassing wisdom and detailed care for our needs. From this key point, God allowed me to peek into a vision of a God-centered culture that reflects the message of the whole Bible. Praise God that one simple way does exist and that He has given it and had it written down for us right from the beginning. I invite you on this journey so you also will share the excitement of knowing His will.

CHAPTER 3

That Which Was Good

And God saw that it was good. (Genesis 1:31)

Then the LORD answered Job out of the storm and said: "Who is this that darkens my counsel with words without knowledge? Brace yourself like a man; I will question you, and you shall answer me. Where were you when I laid the earth's foundation? Tell me, if you understand. Who marked off its dimensions? Surely you know! Who stretched a measuring line across it? On what were its footings set, or who laid its cornerstone - while the morning stars sang together and all the angels shouted for joy?" (Job 38:1-7)

I was twenty-five when the church entrusted me with a small project—building a portable offering box. I put all my heart into designing and constructing it. In 2015, thirty-four years later, I visited that church and saw that box still in use in a high-traffic location and still shining with the special features I had built into it. As I cherished my creation, I realized some important things about creativity and the appreciation of a creator. I saw my character and spirit in that box. I was honored to see it functioning as I had designed it to function. I received joy and satisfaction and wanted to brag about my little creation. I realized then that the happiness and honor we feel when we see the results of our creativity are elements of God's image He built into us.

God was delighted when He observed His crowning creation that bore His image. I did not ponder much this characteristic of humanity until one day in April 1983. I marveled in surprise when the doctor delivered our firstborn and I saw that she looked so much like me. There is a need to dwell on God's "very good" comment after He created Adam. As God shared that part of His image with us—the ability and willingness to praise and receive it—He intended that we would look on all He does and share the same gratitude toward the praiseworthy One Himself. We were actually created for seeing, realizing and responding in appreciation to the goodness of all God had created, and all these actions are sum up in the word: worship.

We can appreciate the superlative comment over the other days of creation knowing that no other created beings bore God's image. We can be certain that God particularly loved Adam. Just as I would not like to see my offering box unused and as much as I could never allow my little daughter to be harmed, God cannot tolerate Adam being harmed, damaged or snatched away.

God had His perfect will for Adam and Eve and for all humanity. He wanted from the beginning to build relationships between Him and for humans to build harmonious, pleasing, loving, and fulfilling relationships among themselves. That should demonstrate God's perfection in His handiwork. Good relationships are actually blessings from God's original design before creation. They are not an afterthought, nor were they only available after Christ's redemption.

I believe the idea of proper human relationships and our spiritual connection with God existed even before creation. Humanity with its beautiful relational potential is one of the great characteristic lights that should shine for God. The goodness in the God-man relationship and interhuman relationships testifies to God's generosity, grace, wisdom, power, love, and praiseworthiness. A light-shining loving culture was part of His original plan.

We are of course not certain how much Adam and Eve knew of God's will apart from the simple instructions He gave them in the garden. We gather bits and pieces of what God desired in Genesis and Exodus, but none of these pieces can compare to the clarity of God's will as stated in Exodus 19–20, which we will discuss at length in this book. If we dwell on the thoughts with this foundational belief, we will see that God's will is consistent from creation to eternity. Eve's and Adam's fall had injected just an interruption into God's perfectly beautiful and praiseworthy plan.

God created that which was good. He liked it, and we can say He is deeply attached to it. Even after the fall, God was determined to salvage what He had once considered very good. He chose Abraham and thus the nation that followed as the agents of His salvation plan. The original chosen people demonstrated the theology, and then the Son of God fulfilled the prophesies of the Old Testament. Then, a new and real chosen people emerged to restore God's joy.

Restoring God's Joy

> But you are a Chosen People, a royal priesthood, a holy nation, a people belonging to God, that you may declare the praises of him who called you out of darkness into his wonderful light. (1 Peter 2:9)
>
> You are the light of the world. A city on a hill cannot be hidden. Neither do people light a lamp and put it under a bowl. Instead they put it on its stand, and it gives light to everyone in the house. In the same way, let your light shine before men, that they may see your good deeds and praise your Father in heaven.
>
> Do not think that I have come to abolish the Law or the Prophets; I have not come to abolish them but to fulfill them. I tell you the truth, until heaven and earth disappear, not the smallest letter, not the least stroke of a pen, will by any means disappear from the Law until everything is accomplished. Anyone who breaks one of the least of these commandments and teaches others to do the same will be called least in the kingdom of heaven, but whoever practices and teaches these commands will be called great in the kingdom of heaven. (Matthew 5:14–20)

God never gave up on His original plan to enjoy humanity as He had created it. He even sacrificed His only begotten Son to redeem it. The way that was later prescribed to the chosen people in the desert through Moses was only a reflection of His original intention for humanity. The commandments stayed unchanged from the time being instituted at Mount Sinai, to the people of God called to follow and return to their practice by the prophets, to the Lord Jesus who eventually affirmed them for the new people of God, and even used as the standard for the identity of the good and faithful ones in the book of Revelations

(Revelations 12:17, 14:12). We can be certain God had no intention of changing the way humanity was to relate to Him and each other. God's glory is declared to the whole universe when God's people follow His plan and live beautifully on earth. This sums up the meaning of being human.

God has by His initiative taken us who are born into darkness after the fall out of darkness into His wonderful light. He and His old and new work are worthy of the praise and glory, and it is our duty to declare this to the world. This new mission of declaring His salvation grace is added to the original mission of humble appreciation of God's creation at the beginning. From the wonder of the initial creation to the beauty of His grace in salvation, God and His work deserve our appreciation and praise, and everything was always about God and His honor in His goodness.

It seems to be a familiar concept that we have always had a mission of appreciating or worshipping God as humans and as saved souls. Yet, until we realize how we have been placing too much emphasis on ourselves, we will not notice we have actually dethroned God from His centrality in the big picture. In the long historical process of forming our tradition today among the churches, we have made personal benefits and desired outcomes for personal lives the centers of our concern. Much talk in the churches and among Christians is about how God can, would and should solve our problems, fulfill our needs, be relevant in our perspective, and many more earthly things.

While God's pleasure is that the right things happen on earth to humanity and the environment, His big picture is much bigger. His glory and honor are based on far more than what we are concerned about in our lifetime and our known universe or our religious experience. As we read in the scriptures, God's justice extends beyond the human experience and includes the angels beyond the earthly realm and human comprehension. God's surpassing glory that fills and spills over the physical universe and the spiritual realms can only be visualized in part, by faith. This is a great light we are privileged to have a glimpse; and our involvement as appreciative spectators and beneficiaries is required as God graciously willed. As redeemed people of God, we should feel the honor of being allowed to be a part in all these processes and benefits. Thanksgiving, praise and worship should be natural and reasonable and even obligated responses on our part, and all that restores the joy God once had and deserve.

Flickering Lights

A dim, weak, distorted and even flickering light can still hold back darkness. At one time, Christians were taught to be holy and good witnesses for Jesus. Back in the 1960s, we were exhorted to dress modestly, not to drink alcohol, not to smoke, and not to go to the movies. We were to stay away from drugs, gambling, and games that could be used for gambling such as cards and mahjong. The church taught us to examine ourselves by reflecting on the Ten Commandments weekly and confessing our sins. In the 1970s, I attended a Christian school in Canada that forbade boys and girls from getting closer than six inches to each other—that was our six-inch rule. Christians were at one point or another actually shining for the Lord Jesus and trusted as good people.

Though we may think correctly or incorrectly that such rules and regulations were artificial or legalistic, Christians were distinguished and known around the world as Don't-Doers—they couldn't do this and couldn't do that. Many people had definitively rejected the gospel saying, "I don't want to become a Christian because if I did, I wouldn't be allowed to do a lot of the things I enjoy. I'd lose my freedom on Sundays and would miss many of my friends." Despite their rejection of the gospel, they along with those who opted for Jesus knew that Christians were distinctive. These do's and don'ts may admittedly be legalistic, but they make Christians different and bear clear evidence of something. No one can deny that there was in most cases a welcome light shining from these cultures. Unfortunately, these flickering lights seem to fade out like dying stars.

It worked a bit too tangibly for Toronto as a city at one time. A Christian named William Holmes Howland had a vision to develop the city to become Toronto the Good. He rallied the city when he campaigned for mayor in 1885 saying, "Let us keep the city a God-fearing city, and I would rather see it thus than the greatest and richest city in the continent." Because of this vision, Howland was actually elected much to the surprise of the opposition.

Under Howland's leadership, which was based on biblical teaching, Toronto dealt with issues of sanitation, public health (including the sewage system and garbage collection), poverty, prostitution, drinking, justice, and more. Breaking the Sabbath was forbidden by law in Ontario, and Howland enforced it by police. Toronto was filled with churches.

Though Howland was mayor for only four years, the motto helped Torontonians achieve the vision of Toronto the Good. Before 1950, 85 percent of the city's population attended Protestant churches every Sunday. The good city maintained its reputation for over 150 years, well into the twentieth century. Even a simple search on the internet[7] using "Toronto the Good" as of October 2018 still show a number of links. This demonstrates that the good old reputation is not forgotten[8]. At one time, Toronto had demonstrated a unique trait that fits the definition of Christian culture. The populace embraced a biblically based value and behaved as Christians should. The city's many churches were experiencing high weekly attendances. All these constituted a recognizable Christian culture. The famous A. W. Tozer was a part of this good Toronto days.

Apart from those cultures established on faith, other great cultures in history have shone. The Roman Empire had praiseworthy cultural elements that still contribute to society today. So did the Tang Dynasty of China. There is no doubt that the shining lights of great cultures are brighter and longer lasting than those of individual stories or testimonies. Individual Christians can be a light that draws others' attention to God when they live holy lives by keeping God's Word. Yet God's people as collective, distinguishable communities were meant to bear a stronger and longer-lasting testimony to God. Apart from God's immediate pleasure in seeing His creation working as designed, this collective testimony may shine not only for contemporaries but also for generations to come.

Christian cultures that have shined brightly include the Victorian Era, though it is hard to distinguish whether its defining feature was political, racial, social, or religious. One cannot deny the impact the Christian faith had on Victorian culture that spread the good name of the English around the world. Many social reforms of that era including prison reform, abolition of slavery, Sunday school, a public education system, and so on can be traced to the politicians' philosophical foundation, their Christian faith.

---

[7] Using Google.ca
[8] Levy "Toronto the Good", The Toronto Sun, October 8, 2018

Hindsight in the Godly Culture

God's chosen people actually received the Great Commission along with the Ten Commandments. We might be more familiar with the Ten Commandments in Exodus 20:3–17 (all the do's and don'ts) and have possibly overlooked the associated commission given in Exodus.

> Now if you obey me fully and keep my covenant, then out of all nations you will be my treasured possession. Although the whole earth is mine, you will be for me a kingdom of priests and a holy nation. These are the words you are to speak to the Israelites. (Exodus 19:5–6)

God had once again sown a seed to build a tangible testimony to declare His presence and favor. The Israelites had surely become a culture that bore witness to God's presence and grace for a time among the nations. Like the residents of Toronto, the chosen people in Toronto lived by the law of God, enjoyed His favor, and demonstrated His presence to the world. That effect faded, however, and was almost forgotten after just a few generations as was the case of Toronto the Good. Just as the Torontonians who looked back, admired, and recounted the good old days, the Israelites and the Christian church through the centuries desired renewal. In church history and even in the Bible, we can read of many attempts to revive the chosen people and the church and to restore the light that once shined for the Lord God.

Subjectivity in a Culture

Is the light of God still illuminating the world? Let us zoom in closer across history to our modern times and examine our personal experience. Let me begin with my spiritual journey, which I hope will encourage you to reflect on yours.

When I was about four, church to me was all about attending Sunday school and adults singing and listening to the pastor preach. Soon, I remembered many Bible stories, more Old Testament stories than New Testament stories. Before long, I committed to believing in God. The stories back then also included Jesus. I believed God, His Father, had sent Him. I loved Jesus's teachings, and I believed in Him. Then I had great trouble one day when I was about ten. My Sunday school teacher spoke of Jesus as both the Son of God and God Himself.

That did not work with my math, and it gave rise to many questions. The answers I received were simply beyond my understanding at that time (and even now especially concerning the Trinity and a few other doctrines). In my teenage years, I explored other faiths and examined their stories out of curiosity and a desire to choose the best. Yet nothing else—including evolution and other religions—convinced me of the authority behind existence and the meaning and destination of life.

My faith was built on the knowledge I gained over the last fifty years that was influenced largely by the post–World War II reconstruction culture in Hong Kong and the Protestant missionary work then. My knowledge sources include that of my teachers, friends, and others and what I saw with my eyes. There were the concepts and vocabulary used in the classrooms. My daily life of living and working in our home-turned-factory exposed me to daily-wage workers and friendships with them. I listened in along with the workers as the radio run all day with whatever popular cultural programming the media was broadcasting. I was also blessed with a father who was a free thinker. He was placed in the Philippines for some family reason in the 1930s at age eleven and was exposed to American influence and ways of thinking in his formative years. He learned to make his own observations and draw his own conclusions about everything rather than following whatever he heard without thinking. He was a self-initiated learner; though stumbling note to note, he played the piano and the saxophone. Today, I am still growing in knowledge as I learn now as an adult Christian and a somewhat educated pastor from a wide variety of sources.

Yet all these are still finite and insignificant compared to the knowledge that is out there available to me and not counting what is beyond my access such as knowledge written in other languages or stored in places I will never visit. People with different cultural backgrounds would certainly gain different knowledge. We are all products of our very limited surroundings.

As deep or as shallow as our roots grew in the environments in which we were planted, we were all cultivated by a unique and limited set of influences. In them, we learned the language, vocabulary, logic, approach to problem solving, foods and tastes, certain style of music, what it means to be good or bad, how to relate to people, and many other aspects of a culture. Sixty years and counting, is not a short time for a sustained learner, but it does represent only a short time in history, let alone eternity. I do not know much more than what I know.

Before encountering someone who was influenced by another

culture, most of us would take for granted that the world should be the way we know it. But then, some of us are surprised when we meet people who do things differently. We may think that their ways are simply wrong and that they should correct themselves to conform with us.

Christians in Canada come from different church subcultures as well as from other social cultures. The differences in these subcultures may have contributed to the reason behind the anecdote "To live up above with the saints that we love, that will be glory. But to live down below with the saints we know, that's another story." Well, too many Christians could cite this regarding each other in their churches. You might have said it regarding others, and quite possibly others are saying it about you. None of us can totally escape being subjective.

Cultural Formations and Changes

On the one hand, cultures make individuals who follow and adapt to them look as they do, but cultures can be formed by the collective behaviors of individuals who deliberately embrace common values. Many more people are cultural adapters rather than being cultural generators and reformers. We adore those who intentionally form or lead cultural changes in accord with our values, and we detest those who initiated cultural changes that we abhor.

Over time, the Christian church has preached and embraced different doctrines. Subcultures may form when people rally around a particular doctrine. Leaders also invent, learn, and circulate new terminologies to defend their positions and ideologies and tried to convert their rivals. Believer baptism, universal priesthood of all believers, the Trinity, and the movements associated with these concepts are a few examples that illustrate this. The vocabularies of these favored concepts filled the minds of righteous warriors as they proclaimed their causes and sought to increase their influence. Their followers heard these words that crowded out the opportunity to hear words used by groups that upheld a different cause.

Our Orientation

The most frequently used words in a culture reflect its or its subcultures' values and ideologies. Words can be propaganda, but they can also cultivate and nurture. The term *brainwash* does not exist for nothing.

For example, some churches insist that the Holy Spirit's filling and baptism must be achieved and demonstrated by speaking in tongues. This is done so frequently that people in such churches are practically brainwashed to practice speaking in tongues at all costs. I have seen some congregants judge each other's spirituality by the frequency with which they spoke in tongues. Another church would focus strictly on the order and traditional form of the service. People in such churches can also be brainwashed to believe that no tongues should be manifested after the days of the apostles.

Other confrontations are due to subcultural differences among Christ's congregations. For example, it used to be difficult for young people to play guitar in worship music. After many years of battles that devastated relationships and divided churches, the guitar become the center of the worship team in many churches. Some churches even think they cannot have true worship without a guitar and that the old-fashioned organ should be shut down and sold or demolished. Doctrinal and practical ministry differences drew so much attention in the churches that efforts to bridge these gaps became the central agenda of the church leadership. In many cases, churches lost their perspective and forgot to pay attention to their Christ instructed mission—the reason they existed.

For some time in Christendom, the word *mission* relates only to foreign missions because they do not suspect there are any not-yet believers in their own countries. That belief never left them though more and more people from non-Christian countries are immigrating and settling in their country. They have missed the need to make disciples out of the yet-to-be disciples among their new not-yet Christian neighbors.

Most people in churches do not recognize or discern their own church's subculture; they just take it for granted as the right or only way. Some just think of the differences in others as plain wrong or ignorant. Self-centeredness, subjectivity, and being judgmental have frequently harmed the church's unity and mission, and that happens when people are not aware of the differences being only cultural factors.

Reflecting on your subculture regarding doctrines and ministry practices is an interesting exercise. What are the deep values your church embraces? The following list may help you identify the key elements.

- What are the most frequently used words for reasoning or justification? (Hint: words used in board meetings or among the leaders.)
- What types of projects or programs receive the most attention, enthusiasm, and allocation of resources?
- Which few items are listed first in a statistical report?
- What key or common words are used in teaching and preaching or in Bible studies?
- What topics and vocabulary are used among the people when they converse with each other in social gatherings?

After examining the above (or more) aspects of your church subculture, I hope you ask, "Is that what God wants us to be and to do? What is God's desire for us?"

A Trans-Millennium Issue

As it is among churches of different denominations today, the Pharisees and the Sadducees held different values dear to their hearts; the Pharisees embraced the prophetic values of Mosaic Law while the Sadducees held dear the importance of the authentic temple order. Either emphasis was good if kept in balance. They were not in agreement, however, and stood in opposition and judgmental attitude against each other. In our familiar terms, the Pharisees were more back to the Bible and the Sadducees were more back to the institution. Many of us Evangelicals would have taken sides with the Pharisees if they had not gone bad in their development. Unfortunately, an unhealthy, over-wordy culture developed. So many commentaries were written that they and the fame of their authors surpassed the importance of scripture itself. Their doctrines and theology were disconnected from authentic, Godly practical spirituality, and thus the Lord Jesus admonished them as hypocrites.

The history of the Pharisees illustrates that movements and cultures that start with a good and reasonable cause may not finish well. We may believe that our churches have improved on what our predecessors had, but it is also possible that we have deviated from the original great cause. How can we tell if we are doing better or worse than before? What criteria may we use to judge the quality of our ministries apart from the quantitative evaluations that a business might use? Has God given the word?

The Pharisees were still at a loss in Jesus's time. While they held their positions and fought theologically and ideologically against the Sadducees, they had a riddle or conundrum they thought no one could solve. On one occasion, they saw that Jesus silenced the Sadducees (Matthew 22:34). They came forward with that question to test Jesus. They thought they could silence Jesus or perhaps approve His authority by asking which the greatest commandment was. But Jesus was not as confused as they were. "Love the Lord your God with all your heart and with all your soul and with all your mind" was Jesus' quotation from Deuteronomy, a well-formulated answer, followed up by the qualifying commentary statement, "This is the first and greatest commandment." Jesus added a second bonus answer without needing to be asked: "Love your neighbor as yourself." How could the central importance of *loving God with all we have and loving neighbors as we love ourselves* have escaped the attention of these religious experts? Was the heavy load of doctrine and theology the reason they were distracted from understanding God's will? Or was it because of the heavy programming, endless administrative meeting, building expansion programs, financial crisis or critical attendance decline in the synagogue?

My Own Pharisaic Journey

In my early years, I was led to reserve for God a special space in my heart and I loved God and His Word. Even during one of my preteen Sunday school "singspiration" times, I resolved to serve Him with my life. Yet a recent quiet reflection revealed a journey I had gone on just as the Pharisees had.

In hindsight, I see God took me through several different vista points. I was exposed to the Christian faith before I turned four. I attended an Evangelical Free Church and was a student in its kindergarten through first grade. My second grade was spent in a Methodist Church school, and grades three through six were in a Christian and Missionary Alliance Church school, and I repeated grade 6 in a Chinese Christian Church school while attending Sunday school at the Evangelical Free Church. For some family reasons, I stopped going to church as I started high school in the YMCA College. However, I resumed church attendance after three years, that time at a Baptist church, where I was baptized.

During my last three years of high school, I became active in ministries in school and in church. In 1973, I moved to Canada and attended a Brethren in Christ Church high school in the Niagara region.

The following year, I joined a Baptist church in Toronto as I entered university, where I received much discipleship and training. I grew as a Christian and experienced various ministry. I was the president of a CCF (Chinese Christian Fellowship) on campus. Our purpose was to reach out and bring the gospel to our fellow students. I was at the same time a committee member in the leadership in the church's eighty-people college group. I was in the church choir and assumed leadership of a Bible study in a college-level intercampus youth conference.

After I graduated in 1978 at age twenty-four, I served as a board member in a church plant project and was involved in various church development task forces. At that time, I interacted frequently with Christians in school and at work trying to understand how other churches were doing ministry. After a twelve-year career in the data processing field while serving as a lay leader in various capacities in our growing congregation, I finally got a chance to attend seminary in 1990 to prepare to become a pastor. (See additional historical experience of discipleship in appendix A.)

After I graduated from seminary, however, I was hesitant to join a church as a pastor. My big issue was the fear of running out of things to preach. During that time, I led a short-term mission team. I was going to preach an evangelistic message at a local church we visited. However, the local Christians had not invited a single non-Christian friend to the meeting. So, our team of eight stopped everything we were preparing and prayed.

I wondered, *what is the church supposed to do?* This congregation comprised a bunch of kind and friendly professionals. God seemed to have blessed them with affluence, and they looked like fine Christians too. I was neither ready to judge them nor dare to provide an answer from my own experience. As we prayed, God gave me the message for the evening. I preached that message that evening all right, but God was not finished with me.

For the next few years, God spoke to me through this same message. It was always on my mind and giving me insights and joy as I start to understand God and His desire for His people. That short answer Jesus gave the Pharisees echoed in my heart and spirit for my next twenty-five years as a pastor. The four ships God showed me that afternoon during that mission trip provided me guidance on how to be a Christian and a clear direction for my ministry as a minister.

My lack of faith in this God-given insight led me to decide to further pursue this answer in the year 2000 by enrolling in a doctorate program at Fuller Theological Seminary. My approach was similar to that of the Pharisees: asking that trans-millennium question and testing the answers given by some of the contemporary authoritative sources. While I was at Fuller, I was re-examining the answer to the Pharisee's question based on Pastor Rick Warren's book *The Purpose Driven Church,* which I read a few years back. I was impressed with the concept of being driven by purpose and the GC2 (Great Commission and Great Commandment) emphasis.

Then another answer that impressed me was a strategy suggested by Christian, A. Schwarz from Germany: natural church development (NCD). Schwarz claimed that he had found the eight essential qualities of a healthy church by a scientific method. I had such new hope that this could answer my trans-millennium question, and I wished to follow the ten steps in his book.

The next concept really impressed me; it was in Pastor Robert E. Logan's book *Raising Leaders for the Harvest.* It outlined the process from visioning not-yet believers as potential pastors to cultivating them to become leaders who could bring others to Christ, the 2 Timothy 2:2 four-generations passing of the baton.

Along with Bob Logan's concept was Neil Cole's vision of reviving the Methodist notion of spiritual accountability living. Cole promoted the life-transformation group (LTG) concept in his book *Cultivating a Life for God* and the simple concept of not spending too much on physical and management infrastructures. Many others taught me through their books and lectures.

Do you think there was enough diversity of traditions, theologies, experiences and busy-ness to make me confused just like the Pharisees? Yes, I held onto the very questions that the Pharisees asked, and wait expectantly for the Lord to give the answer!

Rekindle and Reseed

As much as we do not like to be identified with the Pharisees, we have unknowingly done the same things they did. In the last few decades, so many authors have written scholarly books and commentaries of the Bible, some of which boasted excellence in scholarship and others great insights. My learning at Fuller was just a small part of the greater quest by the global Christian community that asked, "What's the most important thing we must do in our walk as Christians and in our ministries as churches?"

Even early in the days of the first signs of spiritual and church decline in North America, the volume of sales of the books *The Measure of a Church* in 1975 by Gene Goetz and *I Believe in the Church* in 1978 by David Watson pointed to a hungry mass wanting answers. This phenomenon continued with the success of *The Purpose-Driven Church* in 1989 by Rick Warren, *Natural Church Development* in 1996 by Christian A. Schwarz, and interest in the emerging church in the recent decade. Church consultants such as Carl George also looked forward to *the coming church revolution* in his book with that title.

Over the past century, the churches have tried out the charismatic movement and liberalism and emphasized Christian education especially in Sunday school. Then we tried out small groups, evangelism-explosion, all kinds of discipleship programs such as the Navigators' 2-7, building modernization or renewal programs, worship renewal, meta-church, and music renewal, and we leaned toward the Roman Catholic tradition for spiritual formation. We thrived with overseas missions and social concerns. While some are more strategically macro changes, others are more programmatic micro adjustments. These examples are enough to illustrate we have been searching and are in the same boat the inquisitive Pharisees were. If you are well educated theologically or biblically but are still in the market for *the* way or *the* answer, you are likely sharing this journey with the Pharisees.

Many of the above concepts and strategies actually work, but for most of the hundreds of thousands of churches in North America with fewer than a hundred congregants and led by a single pastor, there is just not enough strength in leadership to implement those ideas. The fact is that too many churches in North America are facing decline. Was it because of poor building facilities, poor pastoral leadership, theology, programs? Or was it lack social concern, poor preaching, lack of services for families, charisma, prayers, or a combination of these factors? Whatever the cause, many of these churches may have seen better days. More than one hundred thousand churches have closed in North America since the 1990s.

In the realm of personal spirituality, we have not been hearing the same expression of love for God in the churches even among the leaders. There has been more discussion concerning careers, investments, materialism, retirement preparation, entertainment, and relational issues. In general, love for the world has grown while love for God has shrunk.

Jesus's light still shines but only on a limited scale. While megachurches[9] seem to be bright lights, majority big portion of the 327,000-plus Protestant churches in the US may not shine brightly at all according to the report. Programs and theories based on incidental phenomena such as Acts 2:41 of how successfully the earliest church grew are historically *descriptive*. Could this may be a good pattern to follow to rekindle flickering churches? Or would there be another more authentic way?

I think the reformation of the church needs to be deeper than following models. We need to go back to the original commissioning words charged and entrusted to God's people. They were decreed in *prescriptive* authority free of subjectivity as opposed to selecting in the Bible subjectively or arbitrarily the kind of success story that fit our subjective values. Even in the book of Acts, there are a few passages that say the number of disciples increased. Why is the Acts 2:41 passage selected above all the other passages and that model elevated above the other methods? Paths following descriptive models cannot be compared with paths of obedience to the Lord's expressed desires. God's light does not need to be rekindled as much as it needs to be reseeded. Rekindling implies reviving success in the past whereas reseeding means going back to the original authoritative specifications not trusting the quality of the past success. We should have the wisdom to put our trust in God's original command more than in the success of our limited experiences.

The search for an answer in recent decades has been initiated following the pattern of the Pharisees of Jesus's time. We need an answer that is simple, but comprehensive and usable in churches of any size. We need an answer that will provide continuity between church life, home life, and career life. The answer would have to be good for mature and newborn Christians alike as well as for not-yet believers. This answer would join pastors and leaders with those who follow them on the same journey. We want an answer that can melt the schism between Sunday and the other six days. It should help us interpret our daily lives, connect the seemingly mundane things in light of God's will, and give meaning to all we do. Above all, we want an answer that comes from God's original directives, not human invention or models of incidental contemporary successes.

---

[9] USAChurches.org listed 414 megachurches, those with more than two thousand weekly worshippers, in the US in 2010.

With these thoughts in mind, we pray, "Lord, what is that one priority we should be focusing on in our walk and ministry?"

I praise God that such an answer exists. The Lord Jesus has already answered such a quest for rekindling. Such a simple answer is found in Jesus's reply to the Pharisees in Matthew 22. After receiving these insights, which support the concept of the four ships, I tried them out on many occasions and in many aspects of my life and found amazingly positive, immediate, and lasting results. It worked not only for me but also for anyone willing to follow its principles. I invite you to join the journey through Jesus's answer to the Pharisees in Matthew 22:34–40.

> After they heard that Jesus had silenced the Sadducees, the Pharisees got together. One of them, an expert in the law, tested Jesus with this question: "Teacher, which is the greatest commandment in the Law?" Jesus replied: "Love the Lord your God with all your heart and with all your soul and with all your mind. This is the first and greatest commandment. And the second is like it: Love your neighbor as yourself. All the Law and the Prophets hang on these two commandments."

CHAPTER 4

Answer to Our Search—The Four Ships

I have trouble thinking like a woman, and my wife has trouble thinking like a man. Though we are so close to each other and for years have wished we could think like each other, we just cannot change who we are. That does not mean we have not grown to be more considerate of each other. I hope mutual consideration will do for you what it has done for us—help maintain a strong marital bond. God wants us to empathize with others. The ability to be unselfish and considerate of others' feelings, however, is often underused especially when it comes to our relationship with God.

Most religions dwell much more on the benefits to the adherents than to the wants and passion of the object or person of worship. The themes of evangelism almost always point to how a person can live better, arrive at a better state of being, or solve life's many problems. As history has shown so far, many Christians have that mentality, which I call self-centered religiosity, in which most everything focuses on earthly things and people in the community. Even when we Christians talk, sing about, and celebrate the hope beyond this world, our attitude remains very much self-centered. Not a lot of thought goes into how God feels and worse, what He desires. As we focus on ourselves to find ways to do our religion better, what God prescribed has slipped through our minds. Even when it is right in front of our face, we can still miss it. Unfortunately, this is not a new phenomenon as this happened also in the Old Testament times. The Pharisees and Sadducees were typically into self-centered religiosity and piety. Because of how well they thought they had done with their performance and disciplines, they felt righteous. Though both sects had the privilege of being from authentic origins closely connected to God's presence in Word and rituals, the rituals and study of God's Word had spawned a new religion quite void of a real relationship with Him.

I am afraid that we have become religionists today not much different from the Pharisees and the Sadducees in Jesus's days. We pay much attention to things of our own concern and approach everything from a human perspective to a point that we cannot see things from God's perspective. Much energy has been devoted to how improve people's church experience. Even the days of the Renaissance, the Reformation, the Enlightenment, and many great movements represent celebrated waves of success of such a pursuit. These movements came and went, yet the struggle for cultural renewal constantly remained throughout history in the postmodern churches. After the Renaissance, Christians rediscovered their identity through the Protestant Reformation.[10] Afterward, churches also dealt with decline and confusion, and a subsequent need for revival developed throughout the nineteenth and twentieth centuries.[11] We still desire today a revival in both personal spiritual lives and commitment to the Great Commission.

In the Old Testament, the Israelites drifted repeatedly from God's commandments as attested to by the repeated prophetic calls to return to God.[12] In Jesus's time, passionate religious leaders[13] had good intentions, but over time, they were derailed by the traditions developed during earlier reforms. Many churches have also fallen over the years into new tracks of tradition that deviated from Christ's calling to be a church. There is still a fresh need to return to the Bible to rediscover the purpose for our existence and the proper focus and priorities as churches of Jesus Christ.

---

[10] J. D. Douglas, ed., *The New International Dictionary of the Christian Church* (Grand Rapids, MI: Zondervan, 1974), 830.

[11] Douglas, 428.

[12] The book of Judges from 2:10 onward records that the Israelites failed to remain faithful to God, God reminded them of their failures by using their enemies, and He sent the judges to save them when they turned and called on the Lord. Here are a few instances of prophetic messages to illustrate the point of repeated corrective actions: Isaiah 1:1–31; Jeremiah chapters 2–10; Micah 1:1–7, 6:1–14; Malachi 3:7.

[13] Douglas, 772.

The Trans-Millennium Question of Focus and Priority

Religious confusion and renewal occurred during Jesus's time.[14] The Pharisees meticulously followed traditions expanded from the Mosaic Laws while the Sadducees focused on the priesthood lineage, temple worship, and orthodoxy. The Pharisees' traditions had become too complicated for their followers. Jesus referred to them as people who "tie up heavy loads and put them on men's shoulders, but they themselves are not willing to lift a finger to move them" (Matthew 23:4). In Mark, Jesus admonished the Pharisees because they "let go of the commands of God and are holding on to the traditions of men" (Mark 7:6) and lacked the authenticity based on Isaiah 29:13.

The Sadducees did not accept the Pharisees because they had a different foundational authority: their theological foundation, which was based on the lineage of the priesthood, left them with a limited understanding of resurrection. They were certain resurrection was impossible and challenged Jesus by posing a question concerning marriage after the resurrection.

A third major religious force in Jesus's day, the Essenes, was a sect that promoted a communal practice of holiness and strict ethics. Confusion was present from the unresolved differences among the religious groups within the same faith based on the same Mosaic Law, and each of their emphases drew them off track. Leaders from each sect wanted their own orthodoxy proven correct and the others' proven inferior.

Jesus's teachings challenged all the three rival sects. In one instance, the Pharisees challenged Jesus with the issue of paying taxes (Matthew 22:17–22) and the Sadducees challenged Him on the resurrection (Matthew 22:23–28). In each case, Jesus led them to approach these questions from a totally different perspective and defused both challenges. Despite Jesus's insights, these faithful religious leaders did not recognize Jesus as the promised Messiah and Son of God. After seeing that the Sadducees had failed to defeat Jesus with their challenges, the Pharisees met to formulate a new question, "Which is the greatest commandment in the Law?" (Matthew 22:34–36).

---

[14] Mircea Eliade, *The Encyclopedia of Religion,* vol. 11, 270, and vol. 12, 564. The two references give a brief history concerning the Pharisees, Sadducees, the Essences, their beliefs and relationship dynamics.

The Trans-Millennium Answer

Jesus did not have to search for an answer because He had known God's desire for humankind all along. It was just the right time to disclose what God wants for the God-human relationship as well as for inter-human relationships. Jesus separated His answer in two parts, but His summary, "All the Law and the Prophets hang on these two commandments" (Matthew 22:40) joined these two parts into an illuminating unity. Jesus's answer to this question was more forthcoming and direct compared to His answers to the taxation and resurrection questions (Matthew 22:15–32). Jesus did not select any single commandment; rather, He gave a scriptural answer. The words "Love the Lord your God with all your heart and with all your soul and with all your mind" (Matthew 22:37) resemble closely the decree in Deuteronomy 6:5: "Love the Lord" and differ in only one word in the NIV Bible. Though the words used vary among the gospels, scholars agree[15] that the repetition of the word *all* meant the total, all-encompassing involvement of the whole person.[16] Jesus's answer summarized the commandments given to the Israelites at Mount Sinai (Exodus 20:1–20; Deuteronomy 5:1–6:6).

The Deuteronomy decree affirms that respectful love is the most important relationship between God and humanity (Deuteronomy 6:5). Jesus qualified His answer and stated, "This is the first and greatest commandment. And the second is like it: 'Love your neighbor as yourself.' All the Law and the Prophets hang on these two commandments" (Matthew 22:37–40). The second part of Jesus's answer echoes Leviticus 19:18: "Do not seek revenge … but love your neighbor as yourself." This part has no clear connection to Deuteronomy 5 and 6. The last five commandments and the love for neighbors, however, are unified in the book of Romans.

> The commandments, "Do not commit adultery," "Do not murder," "Do not steal," "Do not covet," and whatever other commandments there may be, are summed up in this one rule: "Love your neighbor as

---

[15] A. D. H. Mayes, *Deuteronomy, The New Century Bible Commentary,* ed. Ronald E. Clements and Matthew Black (London: Marshall, Morgan and Scott, 1979), 151, 156. William Lane, *Mark,* 2nd rev. ed. *The New International Commentary of the New Testament,* ed. Gordon D. Fee (Grand Rapids, MI: Eerdmans, 1974), 432.

[16] Mayes, *Deuteronomy,* 306.

yourself." Love does no harm to its neighbor. Therefore, love is the fulfillment of the law. (Romans 13:9–10)

The contextualization of both parts of Jesus's answer demonstrates that it was based on the Ten Commandments and that He might have expected the Pharisees to make the connection. As I demonstrated in the above chapter, I believe the Ten Commandments reflect God's design before creation in both God-human and human-human relationships.

The Commandments: Standard for All Time

Many individuals resent limits on their freedom. Opposition to the Ten Commandments came from outside and inside the Christian faith. In *Liberating Limits*, John A. Huffman asked this question concerning the Ten Commandments: "Why so much talk about the Law? Aren't we living in an age of grace?"[17] I once studied under a New Testament professor who claimed that the Old Testament Law and the Ten Commandments were no longer binding on New Testament Christians because "if we are led by the Spirit, we are not under the Law" (Galatians 5:18). Jesus warned against such misunderstanding in the Sermon on the Mount: "Do not think that I have come to abolish the Law or the Prophets" (Matthew 5:17).

In Galatians 5:18, Paul warned against achieving righteousness by perfection in keeping the commandments rather than relying on Christ's fulfillment of the law's requirements. If the grace and salvation given through Jesus's death and resurrection had indeed abolished the stipulations of the law and the Ten Commandments, no one would be found guilty. Further, without a measurement for what is and what is not sin, no one would need to believe in Jesus to receive salvation. Jesus fulfilled the requirements of the law and the Prophets (Matthew 5:17–19) rather than abolished them; that affirmed the validity of the law and the prophets. People fall short of God's standard of behavior and need salvation through Christ. When Jesus stressed the priority of loving God and neighbors with all that we are, He was not inventing something new for the New Testament church. Rather, He just repeated the old instructions found in the Ten

---

[17] John A. Huffman, Liberating Limits: A Fresh Look at the Ten Commandments (Dallas, TX: Word, 1980), 143.

Commandments (Deuteronomy 6:1–6). The two great commandments were after all based on the law.

The Ten Commandments were the Hebrew standard that guided an individual's relationship with God and humanity. God wrote the tablets for Moses twice, but the contents were the same (Exodus 32:19, 34:1, 28). Jesus upheld the Commandments: "Anyone who breaks one of the least of these commandments and teaches others to do the same will be called least in the kingdom of heaven, but whoever practices and teaches these commands will be called great in the kingdom of heaven" (Matthew 5:19).

Liberating Limits: Boundary and Agenda

Apart from the commandment to honor one's parents, the tone and language of the Ten Commandments limit certain actions and seem restrictive and negative. However, the language used to summarize the commandments in Deuteronomy and Leviticus is different. Instead of using restrictive negativity, the language is like an agenda prescribing what needs to be done: love God and others (Deuteronomy 6:5–6).

This dynamic appears in Old Testament history and the prophets; the Israelites repeatedly failed to live within the boundaries of the Commandments, and God repeatedly sent judges and prophets to call them to return. After many of these up-and-down cycles and near the end of the Old Testament period, Micah gave a clear summary: "He has showed you, O man, what is good. And what does the LORD require of you? To act justly and to love mercy and to walk humbly with your God" (Micah 6:8). Micah's statement put together very well the crucial question and the summary answer.

The Ten Commandments are like the rules of baseball; they restrict how the game is played but do not prohibit the sport's objective— scoring runs. Baseball's rules allow freedom for the players to strategize, train, and become effective. Similarly, the Ten Commandments are the boundaries within which individuals can exercise freedom and live their lives loving God and others.

Love can be understood in many ways, and the required action— loving God and your neighbors—may seem too broad a guide. Therefore, the church must understand the requirements of loving God and neighbors so it can guide contemporary people to obey the commandment. The following sections revisit the Ten Commandments and demonstrate their categorical distinctions.

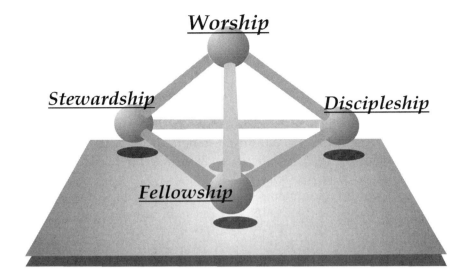

Worship: The First Three Commandments

The first three commandments relate directly to God and His honor, and they set boundaries for what people can do before God. The first commandment, "I am the Lord your God, who brought you out of Egypt, out of the land of slavery. You shall have no other gods before me" (Exodus 20:2–3) emphasizes that there is only one God who created and sustains the universe including human existence. It demands that all people have an attitude of gratitude as they receive life. It affirms that God is the only one who elected and gave special favor to His people. As chosen people, Israelites and Christians alike should worship and keep their faith and allegiance to their Creator alone. It is unacceptable for God's people to shift their allegiance and honor to other gods, persons, or things.

The second commandment states,

> You shall not make for yourself an idol in the form of anything in heaven above or on the earth beneath or in the waters below. You shall not bow down to them or worship them; for I, the LORD your God, am a jealous God, punishing the children for the sin of the fathers to the third and fourth generation of those who hate me, but showing love to a thousand generations of those who love me and keep my commandments. (Exodus 20:4–6)

God established a perimeter with the second commandment and demonstrated how humans could know Him. God wants human beings to understand His spiritual nature, His transcendence of the physical realm, and His omnipresence in creation. Human attempts to use earthly objects to represent God's image misrepresent Him and communicate untruths about His nature. This commandment is an introductory education on God's greatness, and its apparent negativity introduces a deep subject. Within these boundaries, those who seek God can share the understanding of His transcendent, omnipresent existence.

The third commandment, "You shall not misuse the name of the LORD your God, for the LORD will not hold anyone guiltless who misuses his name" (Exodus 20:7), prohibits the misuse of His name. Using God's name in vain is like forgery. Human beings can be tempted to misuse the authority behind a name for selfish gain or to impress others. Using a person's name to do something the person does not desire is an insult and offense and can damage the credibility or reputation of the misrepresented person. Using an individual's name without permission can damage a friendship or allegiance. Misusing a name is a serious offense amid human relationships and injures an individual's relationship with God. Those names most liable to misuse are generally valuable, great, and worthy. People can be tempted to use God's name to support their choices; however, this prohibition requires respect for God's honor more so than how we should respect the head of our country.

The first three commandments are prohibitions and demand that individuals give God proper honor, respect, and worship. They define the boundaries and provide freedom for worship though humans may freely choose their modes of expression. The writer of Deuteronomy suggested that individuals should love God with all they had (Deuteronomy 6:5). This worship must be appropriate and given freely as a response to God's nature and work.

Stewardship: The Fourth Commandment

The fourth commandment reads,

> Remember the Sabbath day by keeping it holy. Six days you shall labor and do all your work, but the seventh day is a Sabbath to the Lord your God. On it you shall

not do any work, neither you, nor your son or daughter, nor your manservant or maidservant, nor your animals, nor the alien within your gates. For in six days the Lord made the heavens and the earth, the sea, and all that is in them, but he rested on the seventh day. Therefore, the Lord blessed the Sabbath day and made it holy. (Exodus 20:7–11)

The word *Sabbath* means desist, rest, intermission, or the ceasing of work (Exodus 20:8–10).[18] The first mention of rest in the Bible is in the creation account and concerns God's creation work (Genesis 2:1–3). The first use of the word *Sabbath* in the NIV translation appears in Exodus; it concerns the sixth day the Israelites received manna in the desert (Exodus 16:23).

The Bible makes little reference to the concept of Sabbath in other cultures, and it is uncertain if societies observed the seven-day work and rest cycle before the Israelites' manna experience (Exodus 16:1–33). Noah waited seven days (Genesis 8:8) between the two instances of releasing the dove, and Jacob worked in seven-year cycles (Genesis 29:18, 27), but these examples are weak reflections of pre-Exodus practice. A. D. H. Mayes claimed, "The case of the Sabbath commandment is considerably complicated by uncertainty regarding the history of the Sabbath."[19] All the examples involve work, not rest alone. The following section examines human work up to the Exodus to contextualize the practice of a seven-day cycle of work and rest.

The Origin of Work and Hard Work

God shared a part of His image with human beings in the ability to work, rule, and manage the earth in Genesis 1:26. According to this verse, work was ordained for humans before creation and is therefore a meaningful part of human existence. This Genesis account does not explicitly describe individuals' working for daily needs but implies that God provided for humanity.

Then God said, "Let us make man in our image, in our likeness, and let them rule." So God created man in

---

[18] Douglas, The New International Dictionary of the Christian Church, 870.
[19] Mayes, *Deuteronomy*, 168.

his own image, in the image of God he created him ... God blessed them and said to them, "Be fruitful and increase in number; fill the earth and subdue it. Rule over the fish of the sea and the birds of the air and over every living creature that moves on the ground." Then God said, "I give you every seed-bearing plant on the face of the whole earth and every tree that has fruit with seed in it. They will be yours for food." (Genesis 1:26–29)

God provided for Adam in the beginning. Adam had fruit, plants, and trees with seeds for food. Man's work was to manage the earth, not to plough fields for the harvest. Before the fall, Adam relied on God for his provision and had no specific compulsion toward hard labor. After the fall, Adam experienced hard work tending crops because thorns and thistles hindered the harvest. God said,

Cursed is the ground because of you; through painful toil you will eat of it all the days of your life. It will produce thorns and thistles for you, and you will eat the plants of the field. By the sweat of your brow you will eat your food until you return to the ground. (Genesis 3:17–19)

In this passage, God started demanding hard work to the point that it became painful toil for Adam to have enough food. While God was still the God of the harvest, Adam's efforts had to contribute in this new provision formula. Instead of a pure reliance on God, there was now a measure of self-reliance required. Under this new circumstance, man's efforts to produce an adequate harvest and his usual reliance on God's provision became a tension he has needed to balance generation after generation. Man's desire to work could have pushed God to the fringe as work became man's focus. Eventually, work became his master and enslaved him as he worked to survive.[20]

The curse allowed in the danger of physical and emotional

---

[20] They took matters into their own hands and decided to save themselves. When they could not do this, they complained about God. That is the backdrop for the discussion of the Sabbath rest in Hebrews 4. Michael Scott Horton, *The Law of Perfect Freedom: Relating to God and Others through the Ten Commandments* (Chicago: Moody Press, 1993), 119.

burnout as humans worked to survive or to amass wealth in many cases. Furthermore, hard work may lead humans to forget that God is the true provider behind the harvest. Self-reliance worked against Adam's trust in God and threatened his fragile relationship with Him. This process can occur today when an individual matures gradually, becomes independent, and feels more and more self-sufficient. Michael Horton asserted,

> This process is familiar to many of us who have seen family members and friends—maybe even ourselves— go from a Christian home, to a disregard for the things of God, and then, finally, to a complete rejection of Christ, in practice if not in theory.[21]

The fourth commandment suggests that the Sabbath provides a regular cycle of physical and emotional rest and recuperation. Emphasizing the sabbatical day as a time to remember the Lord preserves the individual's identity as a servant-manager under God's lordship. This analysis demonstrates that the distinctive and practical functions of the sabbatical commandment are clear and crucial.

Sabbatical Rest, God's Lordship, and Stewardship

Humans understand the need for rest from physical work and the heart's emotional burdens. The reason for rest and recuperation in Exodus 20 is less explicit than the instruction given later in Exodus 23.

> Six days do your work, but on the seventh day do not work, so that your ox and your donkey *may rest* and the slave born in your household, and the alien as well, *may be refreshed*. (Exodus 23:12; emphasis added)

The original command to observe the Sabbath focused on keeping the day "to the Lord" (Exodus 20:11). In addition to the need for rest, the prohibition against work was inaugurated so the Israelites would keep the day apart. People were forbidden to work even if they did not feel the need for rest or recuperation. Everyone was required to focus attention on the Lord and keep it as "a day of sacred assembly"

---

[21] Ibid., 121.

(Leviticus 23:3). During the required holy assembly on the Sabbath, the people were to remember God as the Creator and Lord who ordained work and to recall His provision through the harvest. These assuring thoughts worked to relieve humanity's burden, strain, and stress produced by working for survival.

By human standards, God's work to sustain and rule over creation is immense, but God of course never needs to recuperate from His creative activity. God ordained sabbatical rest only for human wellness and their relationship with Him (which is why Jesus reminded the Pharisees, "The Sabbath was made for man, not man for the Sabbath" Mark 2:27).

Although much attention is given to the idea of rest in the fourth commandment, rest is only part of it. The commandment provides instruction on activities during the other six days: "Six days you shall labor and do all your work" (Exodus 20:9). God ordained work at the design stage of human creation. The meaning of the work and responsibilities that God assigned did not diminish after Adam's fall. The Lord is Lord of the Sabbath and Lord of human work and responsibilities for all seven days.

Focusing on rest alone creates an unbalanced view of the fourth commandment. The reason for the Sabbath decree is theological;[22] it teaches about God's lordship and human stewardship. Willing submission to keep the Sabbath requires humility that demonstrates faith (Psalms 37:7, 46:10). Being faithful and trusting pleases God. God's heart unites in fellowship with humans' when they work hard and keep the Sabbath. J. I. Packer wrote this about Christian worship and stewardship.

> That we must honor God not only by our loyalty (first commandment) and thought-life (second commandment) and words (third commandment), but also by our use of time, in a rhythm of toil and rest; six days for work crowned by one day for worship. God's claim on our sabbaths reminds us that all our time is His gift, to be given back to Him and used for Him ... That Christians are stewards of the gifts and money that God gives them is a familiar truth nowadays; that we are stewards of the time we are given is less stressed,

---

[22] Horton, The Law of Perfect Freedom, 118.

but just as true … making the most of the time, because the days are evil. (Ephesians 5:15ff.; cf. Colossians 4:5) It is for us to make every minute count for God.[23]

Thus, the first three commandments address God's holiness, supremacy, and dignity. The fourth commandment addresses God's lordship. In the context of Jesus's summary, these four commandments address the two identities of Lord and God.

Commandments to Love Our Neighbors

The last six commandments are concerned with human relationships; they instruct humans how to relate to other humans.

> Honor your father and your mother, so that you may live long in the land the LORD your God is giving you. You shall not murder. You shall not commit adultery. You shall not steal. You shall not give false testimony against your neighbor. You shall not covet your neighbor's house. You shall not covet your neighbor's wife, or his manservant or maidservant, his ox or donkey, or anything that belongs to your neighbor. (Exodus 20:12–17)

Jesus's quote from Leviticus 19:18 summarizes these six commandments, and a similar summary appears in the New Testament: "The commandments, 'Do not commit adultery,' 'Do not murder,' 'Do not steal,' 'Do not covet,' and any other commandment there may be, are summed up in this one rule: 'Love your neighbor as yourself'" (Romans 13:9–10). These six commandments seem restrictive, but an agenda of love and respect undergirds them.

The fifth commandment is the starting point for a man's learning to live in harmony with his neighbors. It is much easier to honor and love one's parents as parents are the first ones from whom a person receives love. Returning love to one's parents is an effective way to practice love before an individual begins to establish relationships with others.

The last five commandments protect individuals from acts of violence and mistreatment. Maintaining such boundaries and

---

[23] J. I. Packer, *Growing in Christ* (Wheaton, IL: Crossway, 2007), 252.

responsibilities in interpersonal relationships must start with mutual respect: "So in everything, do to others what you would have them do to you, for this sums up the Law and the Prophets" (Matthew 7:12). They suggest a common love among all humanity. The foundation of these commandments assumes the equality of individuals under God's fatherhood. Expressions of mutual respect and common bonds are included in the concept of fellowship. Fellowship in the name of God pleases Him just as parents are pleased when their children relate well to each other in family relationships. Loving Christian fellowship demonstrates the significant bond among God's people in Christ and is the mark of Christians.

From Prohibitions to Agenda

The Ten Commandments are like the guardrails on a highway that define the safe operating area for automobiles. The summaries in Deuteronomy 6 and Leviticus 19 are similar to the signs and lane markings that provide guidance for proper driving. God's spiritual highway has ten guardrails. As there are only nine prohibitions, the number of limiting rules is extremely minor compared to the vast freedom offered to those who love God and their neighbors.[24]

The command to love God and neighbors is neither a trivial commentary nor a clever pick from one of the commandments as the Pharisees might have suspected. They are principles embedded in the Ten Commandments given once and for all to guide and inspire. They are the essential principles on which the "Law and prophets hang" (Matthew 22:40). Whereas we need to keep changing our new tablets stoneware[25] and have the software updated God does not need a new one! The Commandments He gave were really cast in stone, on the tablets He had Moses brought up Mount Sinai. They need no updating. The New Testament's instructions to Christians are rooted in the same principles. The essential agenda items revealed in the Ten Commandments are to practice God-centered worship, practice faithful stewardship, and extend brotherly fellowship in His name.

---

[24] Refer to the baseball analogy earlier in this chapter.
[25] Current tablet computer products use silicon material that has the same materials in stones.

The Mission: Discipleship

The encounter between God and Moses on Mount Sinai established the Chosen Peoples' mission and strategy. This mission was recorded in Exodus 19, and obedience to the Ten Commandments and the mission were inseparable because one was required for the other. "Now if you obey me fully and keep my covenant, then out of all nations you will be my treasured possession. Although the whole earth is mine, you will be for me a kingdom of priests and a holy nation" (Exodus 19:5–6a).

This priestly kingdom's mission was to demonstrate God's greatness and glory. The Apostle Peter echoed these ideas.

> Now to you who believe, this stone is precious. But to those who do not believe, "The stone the builders rejected has become the capstone," and, "A stone that causes men to stumble and a rock that makes them fall." They stumble because they disobey the message— which is also what they were destined for. But you are a Chosen People, a royal priesthood, a holy nation, a people belonging to God, that you may declare the praises of him who called you out of darkness into his wonderful light. Once you were not a people, but now you are the people of God; once you had not received mercy, but now you have received mercy. (1 Peter 2:7–10)

Peter referred to the deserved praises of God's salvation in Christ because He called the Christians out of darkness into God's light (1 Peter 2:8–9). The content of this declaration is the blessings found in the gospel of Jesus Christ. God commanded the Israelites to attract people to Him, and He commanded Christians to make disciples and baptize people from all nations in His name.

> Then Jesus came to them and said, "All authority … Therefore, go and make disciples of all nations, baptizing them in the name of the Father and of the Son and of the Holy Spirit, and teaching them to obey everything I have commanded you." (Matthew 28:18–20)

God provided a mission for His people in Old and New Testament times to declare His being and His work. Jesus announced His authority over creation and called the church to engage in the Great Commission. God had not changed the mission, nor had He changed His strategy. God gave guidance to His chosen people of old on how to achieve that mission—by keeping the Ten Commandments. The strategy is the same today; when God's church lives out the spirit of the Commandments to love God and neighbors with all their hearts, they too can effectively make disciples in the New Testament time.

Fundamental, Central, Comprehensive, and Original

The sequence of the Ten Commandments outlines priorities beginning with whom to worship and how to perform authentic worship. This eventually affects an individual's attitude toward the responsibilities and mission received from God, and these worship issues affect the way individuals relate to neighbors. The Ten Commandments include an important sequence. God instructed the Israelites concerning other gods: "Do not worship them" (Exodus 34:14; Judges 6:10; 2 Kings 17:35–38). God also gave warnings about being tempted to worship other gods in Deuteronomy 4:28, 8:19, and 11:16. The temple, ceremonies, and priests were installed for the primary purpose of worship because humanity's relationship with God is the foundation of life.

Human failures began with worship—listening to someone else other than God. Adam and Eve listened to and obeyed the tempter instead of God (Genesis 3:1–6). The pattern continued among the chosen people and resulted in repeated calls to repentance by the judges and prophets. The primary messages of the judges and prophets to the Israelites were calls to return to God and correct worship practices. Micah's concluding words emphasize this theme: "He has showed you, O man, what is good. And what does the LORD require of you? To act justly and to love mercy and to walk humbly with your God" (Micah 6:8). A lack of humility caused humans to elevate themselves and accept no higher authority, and thus they failed in granting mercy and justice.

The same failures from the first to the last of the Ten Commandments appear throughout human history from Eve and Cain (Genesis 3:1–6, 4:1–8) to today. None of God's charges against His people were based on anything outside the Ten Commandments; they were also the only measure God ever required to demonstrate the inability of people to achieve perfection and holiness. They are the foundation on which God declared that the whole of humanity would need a savior. When humans are not living like the intended model, they have already failed in their mission of declaring God's glory and will not be able to make disciples for Him.

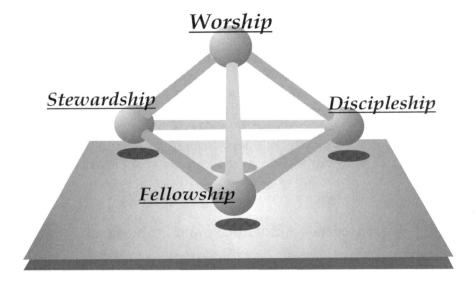

Every requirement for humankind in the Bible involves practicing the principles of worship, stewardship, fellowship, and discipleship. These four "ships" reflect the unity of God's requirement for His people in both Testaments. Humans' failure to keep the Commandments can thus be traced to one or more failures in the four ships. The principles found in the Ten Commandments and the Great Commission are fundamental, comprehensive, central, and sufficient in building ministry in God's eternal enterprise involving humankind.

I believe Jesus's answer was not solely for the Pharisees in the days when He walked the earth. On the Day of Judgment, the Lord will use the same criteria to examine our faithfulness to His charge. God is fair and just; He gave us information and direction so we could follow that and not be condemned. This fundamental calling and the instructions to complete our mission and be His children have basically never changed—nor has there been a new version, patch release, or hotfix. We can be sure that the chosen people of old as well as the present-day church of Christ including God's people in the future are all one in unity under the same requirement. We are all required to follow this great commandment and carry out the Great Commission, and we will be held accountable to the same rules.

Jesus's trans-millennium answer is also trans-Testament. It is not an answer in response to the confusing times and our being lost. It is not so much an answer per se, as it is the original decree that defines the principles of living and mission rooted in God's will and design for humanity. God gave the directives without the need to have a precedent of human confusion or failure so to prove that it works. We as His people just need to faithfully, sincerely, and carefully follow His directives. While so many experts in God's kingdom have claimed to have an answer to rekindling love for God and reviving declining churches, Jesus's answer to the Pharisees stands out like the sun among the planets.

As we will see while we consider our questions regarding ministry and personal spiritual revival in the next six chapters, everything that works will fit in somewhere in this grand scheme of worship, stewardship, fellowship, and discipleship.

With All Our Hearts—Authenticity and Enthusiasm

Churches today and the Old Testament Israelites had similar experiences. As a part of the New Testament church, churches today are commanded to live according to principles based on God's instructions just as the Old Testament Israelites were. God has given us the task of bringing people into His kingdom through Jesus Christ and making God-pleasing disciples just as the Israelites had received the commission to demonstrate God's presence. Like the Israelites who had called for sabbatical assemblies and conducted worship, we worshipped, offered vibrant Sunday schools, taught proper doctrines, adhered to the denominational traditions, and raised young people in the faith. Unfortunately, many churches today as was the case with the Hebrews then have done things in their forms but failed to follow God in authentic spiritual essence.

God was indignant with the Old Testament congregations' inauthentic worship. He spoke through the prophet Malachi: "Oh, that one of you would shut the temple doors, so that you would not light useless fires on my altar! I am not pleased with you ... and I will accept no offering from your hands" (Malachi 1:10). God has not revised His requirements or instructed His people to change their religious obligations despite their failures to love and worship Him. The prophetic message had been consistent, and it called for repentance based on the requirements of the original Commandments and their mission. God has never given any new requirements. Thus worshipping in truth and in spirit means expressing authentic worship and respect for God, being faithful in handling the responsibilities He has given us, loving one's neighbors, and being messengers of His grace. I am confident this kind of Four Ships life is what God was looking for throughout history. It is stated in both Testaments that we are to engage in this journey with all our hearts (Deuteronomy 6:5; Matthew 22:34–40).

CHAPTER 5

Created, Called, and Redeemed for It—Worship

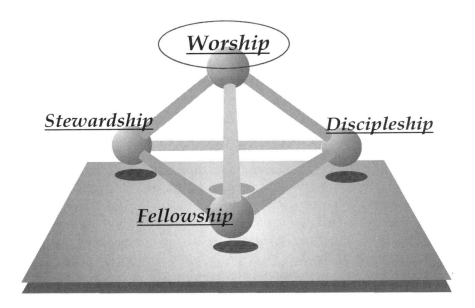

In chapter 4, we briefly examined the biblical foundation of instructions God gave His chosen people. These instructions are trans-millennium and trans-Testament and were given according to the original design of the relationship that was to unfold according to God's creation. These instructions can easily be organized into four areas, four ships, and as we have asserted, the first three prohibitions pointed the way to an agenda of worship. Worship is placed as the first of the four ships for an important reason—because it leads naturally to the other three.

We must explore more fully the subject of worship for several reasons. First, we need to have a clearer definition of what we mean by worship. Only then will we understand that proper and authentic worship is the foundation of being human as God has designed us. Second, the rest of God's requirements in our daily lives—stewardship, fellowship, and discipleship—are other ways of expressing authentic worship.

Third, we have among us today concepts of worship that may be narrow or too exclusive and thus hinder our worship's authenticity. When people serve together with many particular and incomplete perspectives, they fail to understand or appreciate others who approach worship from a different perspective. This creates numerous unnecessary conflicts among Christians and churches.

Fourth, we need to learn, appreciate, and apply the freedom and creativity required of us to worship God. Fifth, a fuller understanding of the concept of worship will help us restore a proper passion for worship. Bob Logan once said, "Evangelism is necessary because there is a lack in worship." His statement helped me understand how much God desires His creation to know and relate to Him.

Broad Concepts of Worship

In the previous chapter, we summarized the first three commandments as the worship commandments. However, the many words and the simplification are never complete in expressing abstract, deep, and complex ideas. After all, it is enough to get some idea in the context, the translations, and discussions. There is no scientific or mathematical formula that calculates the exact translation of the concept of worship.

The root of the word *worship* is said to be an expression of worth-ship, the consistent set of attitudes and actions on the part of worshippers to express the worthiness of the One being worshipped. Let us then approach this topic and study the concept of worship. Worship in its broad sense is not a simple set of rituals that were invented or inherited to comfort worshippers or to let them think they have fulfilled their religious duty. There is always a worshipper and the worshipped; both sides of the relationship have to exist, and it is not worshipper oriented. True worship focuses on the worthiness of the one who is worshipped.

This understanding of worship goes beyond the definition of the word. We use words to represent concepts, but the words we invent sometimes fail to convey fully the ideas or concepts. In many cases, multiple words must be used to represent more-complex ideas. Worship is certainly like the idea stated above. However, its meaning is not limited to the specific, strict definition of such a word as you might know it because I might have a slightly different understanding of it though we described it the same way.

As I mentioned in the previous chapter, the capacity to enjoy, appreciate, and recognize is one of the many aspects of God's nature He shared with us by design. Human beings understand enjoyment on the receiving side of the worship relationship. All kinds of dignifying actions contribute to a growing concept of worship—deference, recognition, praise, being valued, being loved or chosen over others, being remembered, listened to, obeyed, and many others. So we should perceive the concept of worshipping God as the Supreme Being of the universe and His enjoyment of honor, obedience, deference, and recognition in all their forms.

While human worthiness can be measured in relative terms, God's absolute worthiness is marred if His worth is not recognized as supreme, and immeasurable. If we use a concept of price-tagging to describe worthiness, everything else in the world might receive some worth and God would not have a price tag because He is priceless. We may consider many things to be priceless, but if they were to appear before God, they would be of little value or even worthless rather than priceless. But price-tagging may help us if we have been considering too many things to be priceless and have valued God less.

God's worthiness of worship did not start with His saving grace for humankind. He was worthy of worship even before time and the universe were created. Worship is exclusive in that when one subject is worshipped; all other subjects are denied an equal claim of supremacy. The worship all creation owes God is a proper declaration of the eternal truth of His worthiness. This truth cannot be altered by however many things God created. As absolute as God's worthiness is, the requirement of every human being and all creation is to declare the same truth. The refusal to worship God is a denial of His worthiness and an act of rebellion that will make one an enemy of God.

Thus, God must be worshipped exclusively—no others besides Him. This naturally implies that the one who is worshipped is worthy of everything including our submission to His will such as loving our neighbors, His ownership of our stewardship, and bringing others to return to His kingdom. Stewardship, fellowship, and discipleship follow naturally and logically as components of our total worship. It is not that we cannot serve or give honor to other people, but all honor, praise, and faithfulness in service should be done through the immediate recipients and end in the glory of God. Thus stewardship, fellowship, and discipleship should be exercised in the name of and for the love of God and be integral expressions of worship.

Worship can and should happen in every moment of our lives, not only at particular times and in particular places. When understood in its fuller meaning, worship is the center of our relationship with God and the actualization of our being human.

Sidekick View of Worship

Many examples and passages illustrate the concept and specific ways of worship, but I will start with something familiar to establish a basic concept by exploring what we normally see outside of religious buildings. The words *cheer, embrace, praise, choice, subscription, trust, bias, support, passion,* and *love* describe what fans do and have for their favorite sports teams. Each team has fans who for whatever reason choose their favorite teams and remain enthusiastic about and faithful to them.

Fans are totally and passionately biased for their teams. Even the worst teams have faithful fans (short for *fanatics*).[26] Whenever the name of their team is mentioned, passion is aroused in their hearts. Warmth flows deeply among fans as they recount the glories of their teams' successes. They cheer as their teams are winning and bear the pain as their teams are losing. Of course, in the case of God's kingdom and His people, we are all winners! How much easier could it be to become His greatest fan club?

True fans are committed. They buy and even subscribe seasonal tickets for their teams no matter how high the price. They also set aside time and energy to watch their teams and hope (and even pray to God) that their teams win. They thank God for weekends so they can watch the games. They work and live for being fans of their sports teams.

This love and passion for, this dedication commitment to, and this glorious identification with a favored team is a very good illustration of the minimum attitude and behavior for the worship of God, which is a full-time, dedicated, committed, passionate, humble, intelligent, and yet voluntary.

---

[26] On October 23, 2009, Toronto Sports teams were quoted in the *Toronto Observer* as being the worst teams in North America.

Created to Worship

We cannot by logical necessity have preexisted God. God did not feel some unexplained need for something one day, stumbled upon humanity as if it were not His handiwork, and took it for His possession to serve His needs or be His pet. There was never any idea of or need for human existence until God said, "Let us create man in our image." Humankind exists for its Creator's purpose. God designed humanity for Himself and His pleasure. God created us with a spiritual dimension. He shared with humankind many of His other wonderful attributes and imprinted His image in humankind by His choice. Among the gifts He shared with humankind are creativity, the ability and desires to rule and manage, to be intelligent and logical, to love and be loved and honored, to communicate, to speak, to be curious, to have freed choice and more.

Spiritual

The first gift I want to discuss is the gift of being spiritual in nature. "God is spirit" as testified in John 4:24 is a statement that differentiates us from Him and contrasts our limitations and boundaries in the physical world with Him, who is not bound by any restrictions. His existence in the spiritual realm is independent of any physical matter. Physical rules and matters were a new thing when God created them— by His will. The necessary conditions for Adam's continued existence and his physical form were readied during God's creation. At that time, God breathed a part of Himself, His Spirit, into His new metaphysical creation. God's attribute of being Spirit made Adam different and distinct from all other creation. Most important, Adam had a spiritual nature that was compatible and able to communicate with God to share a loving relationship with Him.

Rulership

God gave Adam the gift of authority and rulership so he could fulfill one of the purposes of His design (Genesis 1:26). Adam became an extension of God's authority. At the same time, he was granted the pleasure of experiencing the compliance of the subjects under his rule. We must not underestimate the importance of this aspect of humanity.

Compliance to God and His instruction is submitting our power and authority to His and declaring His worthiness over ours. Our submission constitutes the foundation of worship. The proper handling of the power of rulership is a serious trust given to Adam's worship and stewardship. Turning from the beginning of the Bible to the end, we see that it is in the laying down of human crowns of rulership (Revelation 4:4, 10) that we humans demonstrate our submission to and worship of God.

Intelligence, Discernment, and Appreciation

The human capacity for curiosity is unmatched in the animal kingdom. When God designed human beings, He put into Adam the capacity for discernment. Adam was to be able to tell one animal from another. He was to have dominion over and responsibility for managing God's creation. The most important discernment given to Adam was to recognize and handle certain knowledge and logic. Adam could distinguish God from the rest of His creation and was able to respond to God's instructions in a submissive way. The gift of discernment and knowledge is important because only choices made accordingly will have significance and be of value. Blind, unintelligent, or random decisions carry no significance and establish no worthiness.

Passion

In his song "He's Everything to Me," Ralph Carmichael depicted God's power and art in creation: "In the universe His handiwork I see, in the wind He speaks with majesty."[27]

We may think that the powerful Creator of such a vast, grand universe must be standing at a great distance from His creation and cannot be close to us. However, Mr. Carmichael described his close encounter with God: "Till by faith I met Him face to face … Then I knew that He was more than just a God who didn't care, That lived away out there."

God has never lived way out there and not cared. He has been the God of whom Carmichael wrote, "… walks beside me day by day, ever watching over me lest I stray" and celebrated His passionate everyday nearness.

God desired to interact with His special creation. He gave Adam

---

[27] "He's Everything to Me," Ralph Carmichael, 1969.

instructions regarding what he could and could not eat. He had Adam name the animals. He watched Adam and cared about his loneliness; this transient period of loneliness was necessary so Adam would notice his own needs. God made Eve for him and from him to relieve his lonesome bachelorhood. He spoke to them in the garden of Eden to make sure they were okay. God loved them.

Even after Adam and Eve made the mistake of eating the forbidden fruit suggested by the snake, God held back the punishment due and delayed His judgment for the love of His creation. God kept reaching out to fallen humanity throughout history and granted salvation to all who believed—had faith in—Him. In the history of humankind, God came through by way of His Son in the flesh with provisions, healing, forgiveness, and special gifts. He raised the dead, made the lame walk, fed the hungry, caused the blind to see, and inspired prophets and apostles to preach the gospel to the poor. God's gift of His Son showed His great passion and love for humankind.

Free Will

Another great gift God gave Adam from God's own image was free will. It was meant to be applied, among many things, in responding to God's commands and choosing to obey and love God. The proper use of freedom of choice in God-pleasing ways has been the very meaning of being human from the beginning. Adam actualized his given humanity when he made the right choice according to the truth about God's worthiness. The proper process would demonstrate a deliberate, dynamic, intelligent, and beautiful harmony in the universe as God had designed it. Adam was spiritual in nature, capable, and intelligent; he was free to be passionate in choosing to honor and love God.

We could explore his other gifts in a similar light, but these gifts are necessary for meaningful worship, and they make worship much more valuable to God.

In creating human beings, God made for Himself a wonderful creation He richly gifted. Then He looked at that first man who resembled Him so much and said, "It was very good." What a privilege it is to be a human! Thank You, God, amen!

Before the fall, there was no Sabbath or church rule. There was no theology or denominations, no church buildings, no pastors, no preaching, no worship teams, no choirs, and no congregations. There was no organ, guitar, or drums, but worship—confessing God's worthiness—needed to and must have happened with Adam and Eve's lives. There was no need for the popularly marketed concepts of worship as we know them concerning worshipping in the church today.

Their voluntary and glad submission to and their giving homage to God pleased Him and was sufficient for the first human worship. God gave Adam instructions, and Adam had a choice to do as God told him or do otherwise and face death. There was no need for negotiation between God and Adam. Everything was given with the assumption of God's supremacy. Adam must have understood that choosing the action God prescribed was good, and he had never known by experience the difference until that fateful choice was made. When they did as God said, Adam and Eve honored God's desires, and that was their worship. They expressed the worthiness, the worthship, of God's supremacy without needing any of the elements some people hold dear today. The most important purpose of man was to give God the pleasure of having His supremacy and worthiness recognized, and in doing so, man himself was blessed in the relationship.

Man, Created as blessed Worshippers

God thus created humankind by design to apply all the qualities He endowed them with to honor Him. He was given the intelligence to discern, free will to choose, passion to show enthusiasm, honor to lay down, and a spiritual nature to commune with God, his Creator. This act of glad, enthusiastic submission of our God-given honor fulfills God's desired relationship with His master creation. Proper worship paints a lively and beautiful picture of God's worthiness. The beauty of ongoing worship is God's dynamic and unending creation! Humans are obliged to use these facilities first for their original purpose—to glorify God—though they were given the freedom to apply them in other areas of their lives as well. Worshipping according to God's will triggers the release of God's readied rich blessings for humankind.

Risks on God's Part

Doing God's will may have been the earliest and simplest way Adam worshipped or related to God. God was pleased as long as Adam made the right choices. The recognition of God's supremacy in our lives is the most important piece of knowledge for us as reflected in

King Solomon's Proverbs (e.g., Proverbs 1:7) and in Psalm 111:10. This reverential fear of God is a basic requirement for being a proper human being. The loss of such fear and worship diminishes the value and meaning of any human. For some time, Adam stayed in the blessed state because God accepted his obedience to God's authority.

Because of free will, there is always the risk that humanity might misuse this trusted freedom. Instead of appreciating this privilege, Adam chose to claim independence and refused to honor God's rightful rank and rule over him. Likewise today, we can wrongly use our right to choose and thereby dishonor God. In reality, humankind did bring God grief because all of us have rejected God's authority at some point in our lives in our own ways. Eve and Adam chose not to follow God's command and ate fruit from the forbidden tree. Since then, God's absolute honor has been discounted. In that act of disobedience, humanity declared that God was not the ultimate and only authority. By their actions, Adam and Eve declared that God was not the only worthy commander to follow. They valued and chose the snake's suggestion over God's command.

Instead of doing what they were created to do, Adam and Eve denounced the worthship of God. That corrupted, interrupted, broke, and even stopped their worship of God. They offended God by rejecting Him the moment they doubted Him and chose other persons, things, or desires as higher authorities or better values than God. The problem of lost worship continued from Adam and Eve's time through the days of Noah to Abraham, into the rest of human history, and it will likely continue in the days to come.

Old Testament Call to Return to Worship

We may never comprehend God's redemption plan,[28] but He has always wanted to restore His pleasure in having His created human beings appreciate and follow Him, fellowship with Him, and demonstrate His worthiness. God's passionate love runs deep for His masterpiece creation that bears His image. We as God's worshippers are just too precious to Him to obliterate. God's loss of a loving relationship with man was not acceptable to Him. He was unwavering in restoring His lost worshippers. God has no higher authority to report to and owes no one answers to justify His actions. God needs no consultation as He is

---

[28] "He's Everything to Me," Ralph Carmichael, 1969.

the ultimate source of wisdom. No one should doubt God's confidence in the potential of humanity to recreate the dynamic beauty in the God-human relationship. God knew that humans would very likely make the right choice again using the freedom He had given them. By His own divine choice and wisdom, He called His agents into action.

It seemed that Abram appeared in Genesis just at the right time with the right heart—faith in God. Because of his faith, God decided to grant an opportunity and roll out the plan of salvation through him. There was no explanation in the first encounter story in Genesis; the key factor of faith was explained only later. It was because of faith, the key between man and God, that Abraham and his descendants, the Israelites, became the chosen people. This community of faith called for the rest of humanity to again declare God's worthship.

As God's plan unfolded in the few hundred years that followed, the chosen people were led to the wilderness, where God met them in a way no other nation had experienced before. At the foot of Mount Sinai, God gave the Commandments on stone tablets. He gave the first three commandments to reestablish His supremacy in the God-human relationship. The chosen people were once again called and challenged to exercise their free will with their minds, spirits, humility, and love for God.

Ritualistic worship did not come first in Exodus. Throughout the Old Testament, prophets called the chosen people to return to obedience according to the spirit of the Commandments rather than returning to authentic ritualistic procedures. The foundation and principles of worship are less about their form—their times and places—than about spiritual submission to and love for God and His Commandments—exercising love for God and for neighbors. Rituals or assembly ceremonies on the other hand are not useless as we will explore later. In the messages of the prophets, we understand that the call to return to worship should be seen more as restoration of 24/7, eternal relationship rather than a religious practice to be done just one day a week. Assembled worship is necessary because it demonstrates God's worthiness and cultivates the worshipful life during all seven days.

Evangelism and church are necessary to bring people back to worship God. Church growth is not the end but a means. God desires the church to grow and for people to be saved, but seeing the church grow in numbers and people happy with eternity is not God's pastime. What He is after is the ongoing and unending relationship of love and worship. Evangelism and church worship as earthly functions will pass away when God calls His people to His presence one day. From then on, God will enjoy loving His people, blessing them, and receiving their worship in heaven.

Rituals Help Build the Worshipping Culture

God gave humanity the mental ability to keep some things in focus while allowing other things to be temporarily put aside. He combined this limitation of attention and free will with a rich environment so humanity could recall things from memory and thus have interesting lives.

However, this human characteristic of forgetting also means that people need reminders to bring those important things into focus. Rituals as reminders are important because without them, the instructions given to Adam and the Israelites in the desert would have been forgotten as attention was focused on other things in life. God's regular visits in the garden of Eden helped Adam and Eve remember Him and His instructions. For the Israelites in the desert, God gave the ceremonial rituals and assemblies so the people would be reminded and educated.

Rituals, ceremonies, and regular assemblies are very important ways of sustaining a culture. Various collective actions in assembled rituals stimulate and help propagate the meaning and values during these special times. New Year's days, birthdays, and anniversaries are examples of this. Even commercial, social, or community values today use the way of reminder as propaganda according to this human forgetful characteristic. Many other ceremonies have the same effects including awards events in the entertainment world, Father's Day, Mother's Day, Thanksgiving Day, and so on.

In Exodus, the chosen people received two major parts of the law. The first part included assemblies and festivals such as Passover to help them remember His instructions concerning living God-fearing and obedient lives. This part of the law conveys a sense of His care, love, and nearness.

The second part was the system of sacrifices and especially those that involved confession and forgiveness of sins. This second part illustrates the grace of forgiveness and reconciliation. God did not assume that the Israelites would remember the way of life that pleased Him or that they could live in perfect observance of His law. The contrary was true; God knew the people would forget and would sin. God always knew the impossible outcome of attaining acceptability by keeping the law.

The religious programming for the chosen people was not the ultimate purpose of how people were to relate to God. It was a means to help them engage in their daily lives as worship by doing His will. By their engaging as a community in the festivals, the Exodus stories would be told and the people would rejoice along with the first generation of people, who had been eyewitnesses of the events. These stories would be told repeatedly to their children, who had not seen them. As often as the Passover was kept, they would continue telling the story and passing it on. They would draw attention to God's saving grace and His promise among those who saw and cherished His grace in these stories. Time would pass during each year, and memories would become vague ... and then a reminder would come at the next Passover. Assembled worship is necessary because of our need to cultivate a worshipful lifestyle.

Each festival told a part of God's message in the Old Testament laws. It is not necessary to completely form the mind and practice of a person at one time. Yet over time and in the context of the community, the effects of the stories and collective memory became culturally ingrained in the community and formed a culture that bore witness to God and His faithfulness.

A New Way Opens for Worship

Unfortunately, the positive effects of rituals and assembled worship can be seen only briefly in the Old Testament. The chosen people, like the rest of humanity, were not able to please God completely by keeping His Commandments despite the programs and demands in place. A detachment occurred between their assembled ceremonies and the practice of God's commands in their daily lives. Worship by observing the assemblies, festivals, and sacrifices was corrupted— from the priesthood to the common people. Self-interest took over the hearts of the priests as we read in the two books of Samuel. The people rejected God and set their eyes on the glory of the Gentile kings. Justice was perverted. Kindness to neighbors was withheld. While the worship of God by way of rituals still took place, they became empty and offended God because of their hypocrisy. This failure reflected something deeper—their relationship with God.

The failure of the chosen people shows that by our own efforts, we cannot achieve righteousness and live out God's mission. However, our hypocritical worship does not negate the effectiveness of rituals as a cultivation device. The strategy God uses to cultivate a people for Himself has the most important element in store—grace. Along with the whole system of sacrifices and rituals, the Son of God came in human flesh, suffered, died, and was resurrected to bring sense and meaning to all that was done in the Old Testament.

This restoration process took time. Many miracles needed to be performed so it would prove to be believable for the people in the future. The subsequent Commandments and the history of the Israelites are no less important as parts of that bigger process in history through which God made the call to return to worship. Through that process, the total failure of the chosen people to attain righteousness by the law pointed the way to the need of the Savior.

When we analyze the prophetic messages, we discover that the broken relationship between the chosen people and God had always started with their failure to recognize Jehovah as the only God and their supreme authority. They chose to obey and honor the voices, calls, and invitation of other gods instead of their loving Creator. They thus applied their time, energy, and material resources to serving these other gods. As God's people bent the wrong way with their worship, they naturally associated with those who shared the same objects of worship. Their association (fellowship), dispatch of resources (stewardship), and spiritual influence (discipleship) followed naturally. Thus, over time generations were led astray and God lost His worshippers to the enemy.

Thank God the battle was not over. In this theater of eternal spiritual warfare, God carried out His eternal plan of providing salvation to humankind for Himself. Salvation was necessary not only for the benefit of the saved but more importantly for God's will and the worship He deserved. Who could stand in His way when He was resolved to reclaim His beloved worshippers? Hallelujah!

In the fullness of time, all the necessary settings and players were in place, and the Son of God was given.

Humans celebrate a new, bright future. True actualization of being human is possible again because of the great restoration God has offered. At one point, we were in a broken relationship deserving judgment and death and having no way to reconciliation. But God opened the way through the incarnation, suffering, and redemptive death and resurrection of His Son. Those who are willing to accept

God's offer may again be allowed to worship and become new agents in God's grand plan. Since Old Testament times, faithful people have trusted God for the way of reconciliation. They were considered faithful and were acceptable to God through the same way we put our trust and faith in Christ. It is the way of faith, counting God trustworthy. This is itself a form of worship. Hebrews 11:6 says it loud and clear: "Without faith, it is impossible to please Him."

God's plan of worship restoration means more than reestablishing a religion for humans or requiring them to enjoy one day out of seven. His desire has never centered on human-oriented, practical religion but was always about a much bigger universal picture. There is a deeper beauty of the relationship between Him and His creation and His worthiness that needs to be appreciated. He wants to commission those who are near Him to bring those who have yet to be restored. He desires that an appreciable quality and blessedness of His people would advertise, shine brightly, and cause the voluntary resubmission of those who would come home to Him later. God wants a blessed people for Himself, and they should always have the same characteristic of what I call the Four Ships culture.

Humans were created for and then called and recalled to worship. The broad requirements of worship need to happen deep in the human heart before they can be expressed in their daily walk and regular assemblies. God's call and recalling are precious opportunities He granted so humans could become what they were meant to be as created. To be guided to worship again fulfills a person's once-lost humanity. The chosen people then and now owe God their duty of declaring God's worthiness for their whole lives on earth and for eternity. The worship of God needs to become visible characteristics of their identifiable culture. By our assemblies, by our lives, and by our collective culture after His will, we send a strong message about God's glory.

We must express and demonstrate our allegiance to and love and respect for God by applying the faculties God has given us and to subject even our leadership and rule under God's supremacy. It is of utmost importance to understand this comprehensive concept. If we know God and accept the redemption granted by His Son's blood, it is a serious violation against God's holiness to keep forgetting or refuse to worship. Such blunders and a rebellious attitude are denials of God's worthiness and His deserved pleasure. Those who make such blunders and have a rebellious attitude become enemies of God. They need serious repentance. Having said all that, I hope you are convinced that we must engage ourselves carefully in learning to worship.

God deserves our love and respect with all our hearts, minds, and might. When we worship according to His way, we fulfill the purpose of our existence and are safe and blessed in His embrace.

We must now explore further what we can do to cultivate and live out such an important mission. Praise God from whom all meanings flow!

CHAPTER 6

Called to Assemble in God's name

In the previous chapter, we established that humanity received God's image and was created to relate to God so both sides could enjoy a beautiful relationship. We were created, called, and recalled worshipping Him. We were created compatible with God in His nature to the extent God graciously apportioned it; but we are of course not equal to God. Our lives are a gift, a process by which we enjoy being human while we honor God.

Remembering the concept of this wide perspective about worship is extremely important before we engage in this chapter with assembled worship. Our approach is to start out with a general reflection of our experiences. We will then delve deeper into the heart's journey of worship and discuss some of the deficiencies as we explore the rich world of assembled worship.

The Typical Way of Learning Assembled Worship

With both hands on the handlebars and one foot on the rear step, I pushed my tricycle to church for the first time before I was four. Church to me consisted of great Sunday school classes in which I learned many songs and Bible stories. Later, when I was about twelve, we had our fellowship group and I attended my first summer camp.

My church world consisted of only these things until one day, I noticed that the adults came to church for a different meeting. When I asked about that, someone told me that the adults came to worship. "Worship? What's that all about?" I asked in Cantonese, a southern Chinese dialect. I cannot recall exactly what I was told, but I am sure that the answer was no more than a minute long as my young mind could hold only so much. Vaguely, the answer included the following: they came to sing songs to God and listen to God's Word to show their respect for Him.

In the following years, I participated in worship by learning the songs and following the activities in the program week after week. There was no more mention of how these programs fulfilled the purpose of giving God respect. Over time, my enjoyment of singing and the teachings in the sermons became the reasons for my participation.

I think most people do not have an in-depth understanding of what Sunday services are all about and thus engage in it with little reflection let alone study. That would be all right if we happened to be attending a church with a nearly perfect and organized worship, but that is not the case. Even if you think your church has got it, your experience cannot include other valid and good traditions that happen outside your church. The concept we learn only from experience is not possibly complete and most likely leads to a little misconception here and there. These facts can put us out of focus in our relationship with God. We may even find that the particular values and practices in our experiences might have actually been missing the point according to God's will as expressed in the Bible.

Consider the following comments posted on a website that promoted a book on the study of worship.[29]

> I agree with you when you say that people don't worship because they don't understand it, this was me, but I would like to express my thanks for a well-written study course that leads into a higher realm of praise and worship.
>
> The ... study has changed my life. I now understand what it means to be a worshipper. I will never be the same as a worshipper and as a child of God.
>
> For years I thought I was a worshipper. After going through the study, I realized that I knew very little of what it meant to be a true worshipper. Thank you for developing an easy-to-understand tool that has helped me know what it means to worship God.

---

[29] Anonymous, Testimonials for reading Experiencing Worship https://www.experiencingworship.com/the-worship-study/

We had over twenty people go through your study from our church. Many were experienced in worship leadership. Every one of the students went away with something new and fresh about worship. What a wonderful study for our lay people and those in our worship ministry.

Our church held a study on worship this past spring. Your book was the main material for teaching. I can truly say that people left with a better understanding of worship because of it. Our worship has grown to the next level as a result of the seminar.

It is possible that many people in leadership positions could have learned Sunday worship only by experience. Though they may start with simple responsibilities, they may receive more opportunities as time passes without learning any more about worship. Some people who are wholly responsible for Sunday worship have never done any serious or formal study in the area. This phenomenon can then repeat itself for generations of leadership and result in a church tradition of poor or meaningless worship programming and leadership that may be far from pleasing to God or humanity.

Let us explore further this topic of assembled worship—what most people know of as Sunday services.

A writer on biblicalworship.org wrote,

All around us we hear: Place of Worship, Worship Team, Worship Pastor, Worship Service, Worship Songs, Attitude of Worship, Sanctuary for Worship, Dedicated to God for Worship, etc., etc. I'm sorry (I really am), but I can't find any of these titles in Scripture. They can be found in tradition, but not in the Bible.

There is some truth in what he observed especially regarding the New Testament texts he quoted. However, even if there were a fuller list of scripture quotations, it would not alter the fact that the New Testament's emphasis was pointing to deep spiritual worship compared to what we find in the Old Testament especially in the books of Moses regarding the assembled worship of God.

In the Old Testament, we find references to the place of worship and the Levites who performed various tasks there. There were codes for burnt offerings and sacrifices with details about the actions the priests were to take and even the clothes they were to wear. We also find various ceremonies of dedication and the use of songs in worship.

Yet just because clear instructions concerning ceremonial gatherings are in the Old Testament but absent in the New, that does not imply that the Old Testament principles concerning assembled worship became obsolete with the transition to the early church. We as New Testament people of God must then ask, if we are departing from the Old Testament practice, should we still keep the gatherings? What are we trying to achieve in these Sunday gatherings? What are the values in gathering in the name of Christ?

Emphasis against Common Pitfalls

Such questions can make us uncomfortable because we find security in familiar practices. Yet our desire to please God in our worship propels us in the quest. Let us face some of the common pitfalls.

Personal, Private, and Me-Centered Worship

Some think that worship is no more than a personal and private discipline, commitment, or venture. By negligence or deliberately, there are those who think worship is really a private matter may have ignored there is a personal God on the other end of the worship relationship. God's presence, lordship, and authority are not necessary in their formula of worship. Indeed, at times worship is a personal act that does not even have to have a god on the other end to receive whatever the worshipper is doing in the name of God. These people's worship is quite possibly about themselves or meant to demonstrate their spirituality. These activities are not an expression of their relationship with a real god or about the worshipper's own honor. In these cases, worship is something self-contained and to be done by and within oneself. How can acts like these be acceptable to the all-worthy Creator? There must be a proper relationship between the two sides—the worshipper and the worshipped.

As for those who truly know God, there is definitely a proper place for worship privately as King David demonstrated in his many psalms. Many of those reflect a personal, unshared, and intimate relationship with God. While people can indeed worship God anywhere alone, God demanded that an assembly should gather in His name (Exodus

12:6; Hebrews 10:25). The worship God demands is far more than a personal, private practice. It is because a positive response to God's call to assemble tells of His worthiness while declining His invitation to gather dishonors Him. How can we say we truly worship God if we ignore His invitation or even command for assembly?

Since God had given a call, people inside and outside the community of faith would be watching to see if we as God's people would honor His invitation. To insist on worshipping alone is to deny God's call being honored. To insist on worshipping alone may entangle and bring the rest of the congregation down the path of Achan; he kept things he should not have in the battle against Jericho. That incident caused God to leave the congregation. Setting ourselves aside as God's holy people and being present personally in His holy assembly demonstrates His worthiness to those who find us present. Recognizing the sanctity of God's assembly and being present are parts of true worship. It is not up to us to redefine His authority and insist on being alone rather than assembled. We must do our part to respond to His call to gather. Choosing to be absent from His assembly is nothing less than defiance and is sinning against God's glory.

The people did not initiate assembling and then ask God to be present. When the people were in the desert, God commanded them to hold an assembly so they would keep the Sabbath holy. God initiated the call by speaking through Moses to Pharaoh and demanding he let God's people worship Him. God wanted His chosen people to assemble and worship Him. God summoned His people for the meeting, and He was always present despite the success or failure of the chosen people's attendance. The New Testament does not speak much about having to gather for worship, but the meaning of the word *church* ironically places emphasis on the gathering rather than on what they do in their gatherings. This also speaks against the tendency toward private, personal, and self-centered worship of God.

Self-centeredness is also commonly seen in the attitude of those who demand certain things of Sunday assemblies—good sermons, good music, good child-care programs, good Sunday schools, and good deacons. Worshippers come and demand sometimes strongly that things done be according to their tastes and needs. Having all the above performed well is certainly a great blessing for worshippers, but our call to be present at God's feet is not about getting things we are entitled to. I am not saying we should not ignore and address deficiencies in some worship leadership and the quality of sermons but that we must be careful with our attitude when it comes to evaluating the assembly we experience each Sunday. The truth is we are not entitled to anything. We are not the judges and receivers of worship—God is. Any blessings are but gracious gifts from the hand of our loving Father.

While good sermons, teaching, music, and amenities are great blessings, considering them our entitlements puts us on the throne to be served rather than recognizing the assembly is there to worship God. We are all performers in and contributors to the gathering. We are to put the show on for God, the angels, and the earthly and heavenly spiritual beings to witness God's honor. Who are we to dare usurp the right of the throne while God demands it? Sunday service is really a service session in which we submit ourselves before God with our hearty presence. We serve and God receives the service. Worship is a verb with the subject being the worshippers and the object being the worshipped. The focus of worship is on what the assembled worshippers do for the worshipped, not what the assembly does to the worshippers.

Called to Assemble for Worship

Outside the Bible is evidence that human communities gathered for worship-like activities. Fans of sports, movie stars would congregate to rally. Patriotic people of every country would rise at their national anthems in an assembly. Religious people and philosophers throughout human history have been seeking the meaning of life and most of them thought someone was responsible for human existence. The higher cause which they found would draw followers gathering to pay homage. Acts 17:23 makes mention of such an effort on the part of the Greeks. Though these Greeks felt that there was that gathering force out there, they do not know the one who summoned them. Though we may take for granted that assemblies and gatherings are common, we need to point out some facts about gathering in an assembly.

Unlike random mobs, assemblies are initiated by those who have authority or something of value to offer people. The hope is that the call will give people enough motivation to respond positively and gather. Calls to assemble with absolutely no response are pointless and are degrading to the honor of the one who called for the gathering. Just imagine a birthday boy who invites his friends to his party and thus puts his honor on the line. He will feel honored if his friends come and indignant if they do not. Giving an invitation creates space for expressing a relationship; the response to it provides space to build or degrade the relationship. The more powerful, authoritative, or honored the initiators are, the more motivation their guests have to gather and thus increase the honor of the initiator and the quality of their relationships.

On the other hand, the Bible states clearly that God the Creator who also cares for His creation has always been the only God who called His creation to assemble and honor Him. He summoned the Israelites to leave Egypt to worship Him as a congregation. He demanded that there should be assemblies regularly on Sabbaths, and gatherings for the festivals. Blessings were bestowed and covenants made all in the contexts of the assembled congregation. In the New Testament, the Lord Jesus also instructed the disciples to wait for His presence in gatherings after the resurrection. Important development of the new-born church in the time of the Apostles seldom happened in private but in the contexts of gatherings.

Regularity and Being on Time

We were created with elements that make life interesting such as our ability to remember but also forget things. That places a limit on our ability to multitask and at times requires us to prioritize things. We accumulate so much knowledge and experience but cannot always keep everything in focus. We can handle only a few things of high priority and more things of less importance at any one time. A few things can occupy our attention for a whole day. We thus need a way of focusing on what is important.

> There are six days when you may work, but the seventh day is a Sabbath of rest, *a day of sacred assembly*. You are not to do any work; wherever you live, it is a Sabbath to the LORD. (Leviticus 23:3; emphasis added)

The command given to the chosen people to keep the Sabbath by resting from work and to assemble for worship serves a similar purpose. Even before the fall, God's design and will was that people should focus on their work for six days. At the set holy time, they are summoned to give attention to the one who ordained the rest of their activities. This was true as we read in Genesis how God met with Adam.

Even after the hardship of work was added to humanity as punishment for Adam's and Eve's sin, God still blessed them with one day out of seven for rest so they could recuperate and remember to maintain hearts that honored God.

Thus, joining God's congregation only on Christmas and Easter and missing all the frequent and regular gatherings in His name offends God. Missing Sunday services is not acceptable to Him because He waits in vain and unhappy at the assemblies for meeting and blessing us. As His people, we must give priority to meeting with Him. Do we need to say much then about showing up on time for Sunday services? You may hear from the Lord directly.

Ceremonial Purpose of Honor

God's will was to create such a community—including the angels—from which He would derive and demonstrate His honor and worthiness. The gathering of people or angels creates certain ceremonial dynamics. For humans, birthday parties, opening ceremonies, weddings, graduations, troops marching for inspection, and coronations are assemblies with clear purposes. Worshipping assemblies share certain similarities with such other kinds of assemblies.

God's call to the Israelites was a serious one as indicated in His elaborate specifications for the tabernacle, sacrifices, uniforms, festivals, and preparations all the chosen people had to make to assemble to meet Him. These actions surprise and impress those who do not know the honor God deserves. Yet it is for exactly this reason that God did it that way—to demonstrate to all humankind the immeasurable honor He deserves. The meaning of this call to ceremonies is nothing less than a declaration of His worthiness.

Just as the kind of response people give to the invitation makes a difference to the inviter, the response also causes a difference in the relationship between the two parties. Positive responses draw them into warm, loving, and blessed relationship whereas cold or negative responses cool down the relationship and cause them to drift apart or even bring possible enmity—all because one refused to properly honor the invitation.

Those in the business world understand the importance of this. They hold ceremonies to mark the opening of new branches. They invite customers and business partners to the opening of a new store to build an image and a relationship between the business and its clients.

Likewise, schools hold opening ceremonies and assemblies to motivate students, parents, and teachers for the school year. Weddings mark the beginning of a couple's new identity as husband and wife. Though such assemblies are not the main purpose of businesses, schools, or marriages; they are functions that promote the main emphasis in the relationship—better sales, better education, and healthy families.

Likewise, worship assemblies are not ends in themselves; they are a means to promote God and the relationship between Him and His people. They are times that set the relationship in motion or maintain the momentum of a good relationship. Detailed programs in worship services serve transitional purposes. Even sermons, praise, and worship are not the essence of worship assemblies but are acts through which we express our attitude toward God. Assembled worship uses familiar programs to demonstrate God's honor and in the process bless us with His many favors. These hopes for favors must not overtake the real purpose of Sunday service worship. Assembled worship is about God and His honor, not about us and our desires.

If we Christians all had this understanding of what Sunday service means, criticism of the pastor, the choir, or the way this or that believer was not well treated or respected would mostly disappear. Imagine if Christians were not self-absorbed when they came to church and gave deference to God instead of demanding attention. Imagine if Christians served each other by listening and valuing others' opinions and insights rather than their own because of the Lord. Imagine if Christians humbly accepted and appreciated music, sermons, and worship styles not their own. How pleased God would be if we did all this humbly and in His name. That would turn a congregation of self-righteous churchgoers into true blessed worshippers.

How beautiful will it be when Christians are actively clearing the throne occupied by self and allowing God to be enthroned. In this process they remove idols of music styles, beautiful singers, powerful pastors, sermon styles, and other idols. And they really engage in giving God His due rather than coming to be satisfied. When this becomes true, gathered worship helps us fulfill the first three commandments rather than breaking them while trying to keep them. When true worship happens in a congregation, God is lifted high and everyone—including those who are seeking the faith—can witness His presence and pleasure. That will have an effect not understood by many who seek to make worship—Sunday service—attractive by earthly or worldly strategies.

We have been emphasizing the ceremonial function of assembled worship not only for what it should be but also for pointing a way to correct a misconception that became popular in the 1980s. Many churches hopped on the bandwagon of seeker-friendly outreach efforts hoping to reverse church decline.

No one will ever know the whole reason for the decline that triggered this trend, but I will give you my humble opinion: I think our failure to worship properly caused a backsliding of our attitude toward and performance of evangelism. I think people who came to Sunday services in those days did not have the chance to attend services that actually connect them with God. Among the leaders, worshippers and seekers, very few people might have actually encountered with God. The glory of God was suffocated by the human efforts to attract the crowd. There was very little ceremonial process that demonstrate God's presence among them or that He was pleased with the worshippers. For many reasons, worship services became grounds and events that focused on theologically defending attacks on Christian faith at the time: against liberalism, cults, and the Roman Catholics. There were also concerns such as revivalism, filling of the Holy Spirit, the end times, creationism versus the big-bang theory and evolution, and many other topics. Preaching became the most important part as the sermons did the job of clarifying, teaching, and informing so Christians would believe by the right theology and the non-Christians would clearly know the differences between the conflicting theories.

In the last half century, many people were expecting to be taught new things of the Bible each time they left the service rather than desiring the experience of meeting God as an assembled body of God's people. They were evaluating Sunday services by worldly standards and treating those on the stage and at the pulpit as the performers and servers, and the congregants as the audience and as the ones receiving the service. The leaders were reacting to their church's decline and wanted to use a worldly strategy—to please the audience, and they thus focused on their consumers and somehow left God out of the formula. Sunday services became an exchange between those who were onstage and those in the pews; leaving God standing on the side! These assemblies could only be assemblies gathered in the name of the worshippers and not worthy to be called assemblies in God's name! How should God handle their prayers in such gatherings?

Trinity-Centered Worship: Distinguishing Jesus-Centered Assemblies from God-Centered Assemblies

Another shift in worship that began in the 1960s focused on Jesus or the Holy Spirit rather than on the Father or the Trinity. My conviction concerning the roles of the persons in the Trinity is: we come to worship the Father in the name of the Son led by the Holy Spirit. In this movement the three persons of the Godhead were distinguished, and Christians were frequently led to worship each person singled out of the Godhead distinctly without mentioning the others. One movement has pushed the culture of the churches to a point that the personal Jesus is so emphasized with the focus on His nativity or earthly life, at the expense of His being the anointed Christ and eternal son-ship to the Father. This happened also that some churches isolated the Holy Spirit in worship and forgot that there is the Holy Father. Dismembering and constantly isolating the persons in the Trinity is unnecessary and even dangerous. I encourage an integration of Father, Son, and Holy Spirit in our worship while recognizing their distinctive roles.

The Message and Celebration of the Ceremony

The effects of the ceremonial function are like the effects of miracles. When Jesus was ministering to the sick and needy, His agenda was not always about preaching and proclaiming the truth He represented. The power, authority, love, presence, and approval of God were all represented through those miracles; how the miracles worked was not emphasized. Yet the miracles caught the attention of the spectators and compelled them to reexamine what they had witnessed. Jesus's invitation was simply given and accepted when people were impressed by the miracles they saw and the sense of authority He demonstrated. Miracles and celebrations tell their messages. Miracles tell us Jesus is from God and trust worthy. Celebrative worship tells us that God is worthy!

We may yet to experience the real presence of God and miss these messages because we might have followed a trend that led us to spiral down a path of head knowledge, emotional journeys of (seemingly spiritual) highs, convincing theological debates, impressive performances, and beautiful structures all of which were indirectly related to the object of worship. We looked for the message only from the sermons. The nature of the encounter with God in worship is to be experienced rather than explained by words—just as you must be there to feel the impression of Niagara Falls or the Rocky Mountains. The message of the greatness of God needs to be caught in the process though not explained by words.

The message of any ceremony is the justification for its occurrence, and worship as a ceremony is no exception. We must distinguish the message of the ceremony from the messages in the sermons. In and through creation, God had a message about His greatness and worthiness. He celebrated His greatness with the universe He made. Worshippers are to perform a collective act of delivering the message to those who attend to observe—the spectators (the seekers); worshippers (Christians) are not spectators but performers.

Similarly, the celebration of worship is a celebration of God that proclaims His beautiful works, love, goodness, presence, victory, might, perfection, and other attributes. It is by perceiving the message that those who do not know God and are not worshippers could become impressed, interested, and motivated to seek and know Him. The message of assembled worship is very important and strategic in expanding the assembly of worshippers and attracting and making new disciples. The prescribed Old Testament temple worship, sacrifices, and the law that allowed non-Israelite blood to become assimilated into God's people illustrate this important understanding of proselyting effect about worship.

The message of the assembly is seen and heard not only by the spectators but also by angels, the worshippers and God, who receives the worship. When such pleasant encounters happen, they register in our memories as moments we like to recall; they form the foundation of the close, loving relationship between God and worshippers. If there was any time God would want to hear our prayers and pour out blessings and love on His children, these would logically be these times.

When by faith worshippers proclaim this message of worship, they will arouse the curiosity of those who are around and motivate them to seek God. The message the assembly sends is constant; it always points the spectators to raise their attention to God. Though sermons benefit worshippers, they are not the reason for worship. They are, however, important in that God speaks to His people through them. Worshippers and human spectators alike would understand God's heart and will from these messages.

Worship in Spirit and in Truth

Jesus's discussion with the Samaritan woman at the well concerning worship distinguished the emphasis of worship—the inner person's engagement rather than the outward elements such as where the proper place was for worship. As this is such a crucial issue about worship, we will expound on it in the next chapter.

Having spent so much effort to express to you the value and importance of assembled worship, we can now turn to analyze and restate the functions of the common program used to express worship in our assemblies—focusing on the spiritual journey that lies beneath the religious acts during the service. This understanding will help those who prepare and lead worship and those who participate by following.

CHAPTER 7

Elevate Your Worship

Many have written about worship mostly as Sunday services in churches. They discuss the definitions, concepts, importance, benefits, and necessity of worship; the planning, programming, liturgy, and styles of worship; the art of leadership; the reforming aspects of worship, and so on. In this chapter, I will touch briefly on a few of those definitions and conceptual developments. I will describe worshipful moments of the encounter between God and His people in the context of the very familiar programs of Sunday services. I will offer some analysis and provide descriptions of these encounters between the loving God and His beloved worshipping community.

I hope these discussions will help clarify the nature of worshipping in church against the backdrop of the discussion of the previous chapter concerning the broad idea of worship. My purpose is to provide some insight and a better focus on the matter and lay the groundwork for more-realistic planning and participation. I will discuss some things we can do to develop God-pleasing worship services.

I claimed, in agreement with Bob Logan, in the previous chapter, "evangelism is necessary because worship is deficient." Sunday worship is necessary because of the need to build a life of worship on the other six days as well.

Have You Worshipped?

"Have you worshipped?" Most churchgoers might frown on this question if they were asked as they were leaving a Sunday service. Some might ask, "What's that question all about? Didn't I just finish a Sunday worship? Didn't I just enjoy God's blessing with the Word?

The preacher was just wonderful today. That was just what our church needed to hear. I have indeed worshipped today." Another might say, "Of course. I made it in time for the sermon." But many of us do not really examine ourselves deeply enough to answer that question truthfully. The variety of answers and the questions generated by this inquiry derive mainly from different concepts of worship.

Our Experience of Worship

We go to church every Sunday and participate in the service. Week after week, most of us go through similar routines, but it is possible that what happened in the service were no more than empty rituals. Some people were physically present but left without having had a spiritual encounter with God. Others may have had a personal encounter with God at the service but did not join the other worshippers. It is quite possible that only a few truly met intimately with the personal God in an assembly of worshippers.

Humanist Perspective

Most people do only what is in their self-interest. The humanist is self-sufficient and needs to rely on other humans only in crises. A pure humanist does not see the reality of God. (Sadly, even people who believe in God but have a self-centered religious faith typically have a small-God concept.) To the pure humanists, God is only a helping force outside their self-centered universe whom they summon only in times of need. In their hearts, God is but an inactive something that exists somewhere but is neither influential nor significant in times of peace and affluence. To them, there is naturally no need to relate to their god—no need to worship. There is not really a sovereign identity they can worship. There is practically no God! Christian church worship appears to these humanists as purely cultic rituals in which the weak and the helpless gather to use a common psychological crutch.

Unfortunately, many Christians seem to have adopted a position very similar to that of the humanists without knowing it. They think God is too small to value or is unworthy of commanding faith or deserving attention. They come to worship with a self-centered mindset, and worship has been reduced to some personal rituals to please themselves or find comfort in self-oriented righteousness.

The Higher Perspective

As briefly discussed in the last chapter, God revealed Himself as a sovereign and almighty God who loved and cared. His perfect character and attributes are worthy of being appreciated, praised, and honored at all times. He was, is, and will always be the owner and governor of creation including those here below and in heaven. They owe Him recognition, appreciation, praise, and honor. It is inappropriate not to recognize, confess, appreciate, and worship God because it is for His own glory that He created the heavens and earth. Worship is something creation owes its Creator.

It may sound as though God is greedy and hungry for appreciation and worship, but we must not forget that the words *appreciation, worship,* and other good words are a given privilege for us as created beings. First, we should not elevate ourselves above God to question His morality. He is the creator who owns and grants all rights and defined all morality, and He is the final judge, not us. Then we must realize it is a pleasure to appreciate, and it is a suffering to face and live with things that are not worthy. We should not take lightly the opportunity to see and appreciate God's beauty and perfection let alone question God's self-centeredness. Creation itself is God centered rather than human centered.

God created human beings to honor Him for His unchanging greatness. Humans should praise and honor Him for His magnificent being and be thankful for and appreciate the love and grace He shows us. A. W. Tozer gave a very meaningful description of the nature of worship, which I paraphrase here: to feel in the heart and express in some appropriate manner in a humbling but delightful sense of admiring awe and astonished wonder.

Warren Wiersbe in his book *Real Worship* pointed out, "Worship involves WONDER!" Wonder is an internal reaction of a person to some external event. The reaction can be caused by what the person perceives through the senses. It can result from a person's perception of God's greatness and beauty. Wonder is the initial requirement for worshipping God because of His being and what He can do in His holy love. The feeling of wonder is not an act of worship. We must out of wonder acknowledge that God is the great one behind the perceived wonder and express that He is worthy of praise through some action.

Worship Paints a Picture of God

What we do during worship conveys our feelings about God to all the people there. Some people form their concept of God from what they experience at Sunday services. When the congregation sings hymns of praise half-heartedly or the words come out without confidence or conviction, that presents a God who is not worthy of praise. A. W. Tozer described worship in church as a missing jewel of the evangelical church, and he did not overstate the problem. Worship with its benefits for humans should certainly be a jewel, but the church has missed seeing this privilege and has somehow become satisfied with superficial things. How does worship happen in most churches? Let us explore.

Call to Worship

In her powerful book *Up with Worship*, Anne Ortlund correctly suggested that even Christians don't worship naturally. Though we think in theory they should know how to worship, they still have to be taught and then prompted and reminded to worship. Many are fit to approach only the all-loving God, not the all-mighty or the all-holy God. People need reminding, prompting. People today tend to be naturally unaware of the seriousness of their encounters with the Almighty. They need somebody to help them prepare for proper worship of the Almighty.

They need a proper call to make a congregation aware of the corporate activity about to take place. They must leave all cares of the world, even the work for God in many cases, and prostrate themselves, at least in spirit, before God. Without such a call, they risk being spiritually unconscious, which can hinder worship or make it unacceptable to God.

When a proper call to worship is made, the people of God will be prepared and may be ready just as a bride is ready for her wedding. God is honored through the heart-deep responses of His people to respect His worth, dignity, and greatness as they approach Him individually and as an assembly.

In the Music

When done collectively, music brings unity and makes a common statement. Voices do not come from passive observation. We can participate physically but not necessarily mentally or spiritually. But in singing, we can express unity and affirm God's worth. Music calls for a certain format, rhythm, and emotional level that are helpful for expression.

In our Sunday worship experience, we sing songs and hymns, some of which address God in the second person—"Thou" or "You." When we sing these with our minds and hearts, we can speak to God directly in faith and through Jesus's name. We utter words of praise and adoration such a "Holy, Holy, Holy, Lord God Almighty; Early in the morning our songs shall rise to Thee." Such direct address acknowledges He is holy and worthy of recognition. We sing to Him instead of telling others about Him.

Singing directly to God, however, does not guarantee valid communication. Many times, God—the object of communication—is out of focus and even out of mind because Many times, the beauty of music or the singing environment will fill our sight and God is crowded out of sight. People who do not focus on God in worship services tend to utter the words without attaching their minds and hearts to them. When their minds are not with them, it is quite likely that their spirits are not participating in the singing as well. Words uttered or songs sung that way are just superficial religious rituals that do not contribute to worship. Amos and other prophets revealed God's assessment of these kinds of actions as false religion that He hated.

Congregants can join their hearts and minds and sing together truthfully and joyously celebrating God's goodness, faithfulness, beauty, and honor. By praising His power, the wonders of His deeds, and His wisdom, they show reverence and respect for Him. A conscious true heart's journey is thus necessary for singing in church worship. When people pour out their hearts in thunderous voices, unite in prayerful whisper in songs of confession, and earnestly sing, "Heavenly Father, We adore you!" that is when God receives recognition as the Lord and receives glory. That is the time the congregation has worshipped.

The congregants' minds and spirits can actually feel God listening attentively. In response, they sing with increased enthusiasm and energy. Have you had such times when you knew God was listening to you personally and corporately? In such times, you are aware of His presence and are almost conversing with Him in songs that pledge allegiance and faithfulness with communication between God and the whole church. What honor for God!

Other times, we address God in our songs with third-person

pronouns—"Him," "His," and so on. Worship encounter is induced indirectly instead of directly in using these third-person songs. In the song "Praise Him! Praise Him! Jesus Our Blessed Redeemer," we do not address Him directly; rather, we proclaim to each other pronouncing His worthiness of praise. As we sing God's worth by reciting His work and grace, we agree in our hearts with what others have sung about God. Worship happens then but in a different way. We are induced to voice the prayer in our hearts with true thanksgiving, appreciation, and awe.

Worship can happen to a fuller and richer extent only when our hearts respond when we sing these third-person hymns. God is pleased when He is talked about in the third person or addressed directly; both are true worship.

The worship teams (music teams in most cases these days) and choirs serve a similar role as the congregation does in singing songs to each other. They enhance the statement about God's dignity by producing a more beautiful and professional music. Their work is more than doing beautiful music for music's sake. They are responsible for leading the congregation in singing with their hearts as well as their voices. They are models for the congregation; they add life and beauty to worship as did the singing Levites.

When musicians and choirs take their roles seriously and focus their ministry on the glory and heartfelt worthiness of God, we have a true worship in them. When the people respond to their mood, are induced to praise and wonder, and are inspired to cheer for God's glory and beauty, the worship of God has occurred.

Worship practice has changed much over the last thirty years especially in regard to music. Forty or so years ago, there was no lack of spiritual songs that expressed a person's desire to seek God and paint the beauty of a godly spiritual journey. These old hymns did not really address God directly and say, "We worship you." As a worship song leader,[30] I had a hard time choosing more-direct worshipping hymns. I asked God for someone to write more of such songs. Today, we have almost exclusively worship-oriented songs used in Sunday service. Much of the spirit-influencing old hymns have been forgotten. Worship song libraries seem to be driven by the market and popularity more

---

[30] I do not describe myself as worship leader because the ushers and the others who are up front or backstage, including the preacher and the one who made the bulletin publication, are also all worship leaders.

than by the merits of the lyrics or the music. Congregation members have a hard time keeping up with learning the songs and have in too many cases become audiences at praise-and-worship time. There needs to be a more educated balance in selecting hymns and postmodern praise-and-worship songs so congregants can sing together, worship, and be led into spiritual paths with God not only during services but also during their daily living.

I was exposed early in life to traditional (in terms of my generation) church music; the over six hundred old songs[31] I know are truly a spiritual and musical treasure too big to throw away. Our typical hymnbook contains four hundred to seven hundred songs and hymns written by hundreds of songwriters; the music is really the precipitation of thousands of pieces written earlier. These songs have endured the test of time, and many would fade into obscurity in church and music history. Yet today, our worship teams would pick up selections from the work of a few songwriters driven mostly by popularity and marketing channels before their works were tested in time. Our congregations are thus under the influence of a few new stars but have passed up time-proven treasures.

I have witnessed many times even new believers and postmodern Christians participating well in singing; they have told me they find spiritual connection and edification as well as worship in these old treasures. This un-reflected trust only in market-driven or popular new songs has squeezed out the treasures of our heritage. That takes away the depth, enthusiasm, and dynamism in congregational singing. When congregants are not engaged in singing their hearts out but are just spectators, song leaders should consider their ministry a failure. The hearts of those who are only audience members may not even connect with songs well and can easily drift away instead of being led to worship. Then what does God get from His worshippers? This pains Him and the angels when worship was supposed to bring them pleasure.

In the Language

Words reflect the relationship between the parties involved in communication. There is a language for the back alleys, for the courts, for the marketplace, and for our relationship with God. We may have

---

[31] Including religious songs and secular music.

witnessed people converse in such a way that causes people to stare at them. A husband and wife who look like a pair of true lovers may shift their language into argument when they are alone. We use language that differs in tone and vocabulary in different aspects of our relationships.

The language used must represent not only the human side of the encounter but also God, who is eager to speak to us, His beloved. Language in worship should not be too deliberately degrading or artificially lofty that it creates a discontinuity between God and the worshippers' culture. There is a language for each individual congregation. Most appropriate would be language that helps people feel an upward movement toward God as they approach His throne. We should choose words and construct sentences only after careful consideration. Rehearsal may be necessary until everything the worship leaders say becomes natural and transparent to the worshippers. The artistry and demonstrated honor will invite worshippers to follow in an attitude that reflects the dignity and honor of the leaders.

When this matching echo in attitude and worship takes place, the words of the human leaders become the congregation's words. The prompting of the leader should convey the prompting of the Holy Spirit, and it is then that we respond to God, He speaks to us, and we have a true, God-pleasing encounter. Worship spreads from the leader to the congregation, and God accepts the service of the whole congregation rather than just that of the leaders. When that happens, even people who do not have the God-human intimacy will feel God's presence. And body language can have the same effect. We can gracefully balance the expressions of our hearts with dignified moves. Rude, ill-mannered, and disrespectful body language is unacceptable; those who exhibit it withhold their best from God.

In Prayer

When words of prayer truly represent the voices of the people, they can join in and respond with a heartfelt amen. When God is spoken to in such honest terms without half-hearted hitchhiking in corporate prayers, He is honored and recognized as the almighty and caring God who listens to His people. He is then pleased and honored. Worship is happening!

Prayer leaders should carefully plan and prepare. Half-heartedness, absentmindedness, and lack of unity in thoughts often hinder

90

meaningful corporate prayer. No matter how much experience they have, prayer leaders must not take leading prayer lightly for they are representing the people in front of almighty God and should engage with God during their preparation. They should examine their congregations and formulate appropriate relational positions between God and the people. People are more sensitive to the Holy Spirit's guidance if they spend time writing their prayers. Writing their prayers from their hearts word for word and rehearsing them worshipfully are respectful practices. They should lead prayer being true to their own hearts while representing the congregants. Unprepared prayers in worship tend to be repetitive, irrelevant, scattered, and distracting.

In the Confession of Sin

Evangelical churches are possibly lagging behind Roman Catholic churches in the spiritual discipline of sin confession in assembled worship. Personal and corporate confessional prayers should not be confused with the statement in which the church says aloud its theological conviction. The confession of sin constitutes true worship more than many of us in the evangelical circle think. Personal and corporate (Nehemiah 9) confessional prayer prompts worshippers to reflect on their lives in front of God's holiness.

With the absence of such practice, we in fact are fooling ourselves in front of the all-knowing God. God is never fooled. The lack of the opportunity to be brought right up to God's throne allowed too many Christians to stay in sin, and their spiritual lives remain untransformed for long periods because of their lack of awareness of God's holiness and their sinfulness. I believe this has become a stumbling block for people's spiritual journeys toward God and has marred God's glory and honor. When a congregation has the time for such sin confession, their attention is drawn to confront God's omnipresence and omniscience and to recognize His holiness. This recognition is pleasing to God and is an act of beautiful fragrance offered to Him as worship. These all contribute to God's honor—sinners' willingness to confront their sin and throw themselves at the cross to ask for forgiveness. The inner action of the hearts catalysts a turning point to obey God's holy way, commitment to repentance and any needed restitution to people they sinned against. When we confess, we draw closer to God and God draws close to us. A beautiful, intimate, spiritual encounter plays out in the universe, and God is honored. True sin confession helps

Christians enter acceptable worship and contributes greatly to their spiritual formation and reformation. Failure to worship by confession causes difficulties too in evangelism. I think we should once again emphasize this important spiritual discipline in our Sunday services. People who participated in such a congregation would not miss the spiritual advancements of individuals and would bear witness to God's presence and holiness; that would give God the glory for what they see in His people!

In Quietness

Anne Ortlund described our need to be still before God because we can worship God by being quiet. The world tells us, "Don't just stand there—do something!" Yet God demands that we be still and know He is God: "Don't just go around doing things! Take off your shoes and stand still!" Our society never wants to stand still. We are so busy that our minds are over-occupied. Since worship demands our whole being and energy, we cannot keep ourselves busy and be attentive to God at the same time. Conversing with and worshipping Him demands stillness and attention. How dignified it is for God to speak in a still, small voice to a united, quiet, attentive, and expectant congregation. When the prompter stills the congregation to shift their focus to God, the congregants may respond in silence to admit, express, and admire God's honor, dignity, and beauty. God is glorified, and worship has taken place.

In Offering of the Gifts

The primary motive of the gift in worship is neither helping the needy nor financing the church. We cannot totally separate the giving of money from the financial needs of the institution, but the healthier view of offering money is considering it an honoring of the host of worship by a gift. Empty-handedness makes a statement of indifference or cold-heartedness while bringing a gift demonstrates love and respect for the host. Willing, glad, and enthusiastic gifts are acts of worship; worshippers must offer their gifts in a spirit of reverence for God so their gifts will be true expressions of their love and respect.

Nothing given to God should be given as a tip or a payment for a blessing at bargain-basement prices. When God's people are truly moved by His love and kindness, they will know there is no price that could be put on it. They know they can never repay God for His priceless gifts. Thus, they set aside a generous portion of their possessions mindful that this act is a demonstration of their love, respect, and honor for God.

The congregation should of course give more than money. Their disciplines in life and their successes and victories during the week are valid, acceptable, and pleasing offerings. When the whole group participates in worship by offering tangible as well as intangible gifts consciously and prayerfully, they enter into a meaningful spiritual encounter with God and corporate worship occurs.

Through the Word of God

The Word of God is a very important part of worship in most churches. It can be read or preached in a proclamation. The quality of the readers' ministry affects the likelihood of corporate worship, but no matter how expertly done, reading is not in and of itself an act of corporate worship. Likewise, with sermons. When leaders perform their tasks well, the ministry can become their personal worship during services, but the quality of the preached material or the skill with which they deliver it is not an act of corporate worship. Rather, it is the corporate response of the congregation that may become corporate worship.

When the Holy Spirit speaks to the hearts of listeners through the words read or preached, the people will begin to interact with God with their own spirits. They can then engage with the message of the Word and may come to a point that they submit to God's message and obey it and pray aloud or in silence. It is then that God receives His honor and glory. It is then that God's lordship is recognized. It is then that the Holy Spirit is happy within the believer and God receives the thanksgiving of His people. Then, the real, intimate encounter between the loving God and His precious church happens in the way He intended. This is the most pleasant time for God to pour out His joy, peace, and love to the church and to each believer individually. It is then that nonbelievers can witness the presence of God and His Holy Spirit.

What Really Causes Worship

Worship occurs when people are stimulated to perceive God and His grace and work and are prompted to wonder. When their hearts and spirits feel God's presence, through faith, people respond by expressing their hearts and spiritual emotions by means of the various programs we are familiar with. Worship happens as a continuous dialogue and encounter throughout the service. The actual participants may vary a little because some of the people may not have the true feeling at certain times, but worship does happen.

I want to share a few more observations to capture what happens in a person and what is involved in bringing about worship in these programs.

Remember His Loving-Kindness

Worship happens in conjunction with human memory. Recalling the grace and loving-kindness God has shown us involves our memory. How can we have a heart of thanksgiving unless we remember what God accomplished for our benefit? Without the recollections, we would not appreciate our former woeful situation or the help we received from God. To help people worship, worship leaders should stimulate memories of God and His benefits. Sights, sounds, and smell can stimulate our memory too.

Your Mind Matters

Let me borrow the title of one of John R. W. Stott's books, *Your Mind Matters*. Worship must involve the mind; without it, there can be no truthfulness or wonder. Knowledge of God is to be reflected and digested. Contemplation, appreciation, and wonder are activities of the mind. People cannot worship without involving their minds.

Your Body Matters Too!

Our bodies are the foundation of first-level communication. The mind perceives sounds, sights, and smells. When the body is tired, the mind wanders and there is little chance that our spirits are active. Many times, body language is a deeper and truer expression than our words are.

Your Faith and Spiritual Consciousness Matters

"Without faith, it is impossible to please Him, for he that comes to God must believe that HE IS, and that He rewards those who diligently seek Him" (Hebrews 11:6). Faith pleases God. Every spiritual encounter requires faith because of its nonphysical character. We can allow our inner person to be set free so we can explore God's richness not by our physical sight or touch but by the eyes of our spirit and hands of our faith. Contact has transpired through physical sights, sounds, and other senses. Our spiritual person becomes alive with faith. The spirit in us is awakened and is aware of what is happening in the spiritual realm. Faith connects our minds and spirits to God's Spirit. Faith allows us to see things in God's realm. God is pleased when congregations are stimulated into active faith in approaching Him through the only way, Jesus Christ, in trusting God's presence.

When Worship Happens

When worship happens, God draws nearer to His people as He promised. I believe the faithful and not-yet believers alike can feel His presence. In Old Testament times, Joseph, the son of Jacob, and Daniel the prophet were described as men in whose lives the people of their generation could witness the Spirit's presence. In the time of the early church, the church was described as having favor in the eyes of the people because of God's presence with them.

Many times, churches are worried that nonbelievers may not hear the gospel after they leave the building. Thus, these churches sacrifice the time of worship to run evangelistic efforts. Their songs, scripture readings, music, and preaching are directed at proclaiming the gospel to any nonbeliever's present. That is a valid activity at all other times and sometimes even during worship, but consistently taking God's glory time to evangelize is like a wife who keeps showing off the gifts her husband gave her to others while neglecting to spend time with him in intimacy.

In the case of God and His church, the worship encounter itself witnesses to His reality and the relationship between Him and His people. Worship is an extremely effective witness. We can preach the gospel as much as we want, but without proper worship, nonbelievers will listen, be convinced but not impressed. When true worship happens and they see God among His people, they will be drawn to Christ and ask, "How can I know Him too?"

When worship occurs not in one or two parts of a service but in continuous harmony and in a natural flow, it resembles a skillful ping-pong game: God speaks, and the people respond; they praise God, and He responds. Heaven on earth! We can all feel the transforming power of worship. When that happens who would want anything else on Sunday?

Are you having problems with latecomers? Absenteeism? People missing daily devotion? Lacking commitment? Private faith without the motivation to share it with others? Worship itself will not solve all these problems, but it would be hard to explain how these things could happen in the face of genuine, exuberant worship.

Churches often have the 20/80 problem—20 percent of the people do 80 percent of the work. I believe this phenomenon is related to the 80 percent's lack of encounters with God. After a genuine encounter with Him, who would not respond to Him in awe and reverence and apply themselves in His service? Isaiah saw God on His throne and responded. I think most of us would too even if it were not to the same extent as it was for Isaiah. Worship is the hub of all ministries of the church.

When people worship, they are likely to respond to God's teaching and the calls for training. Corporate worship encourages people to keep up personal devotion and personal worship. Worship in which there is an encounter with the Almighty helps build a worshipful and God-fearing lifestyle. Recognition of God's lordship and fatherhood move people into ministries where they worshipfully exercise their gifts.

A worshipful church is a church of clear witness, a church full of power, a church that exhibits the life abundant, a church that is effective, a church that develops the fuller potential of its members' gifts, a church after God's heart. When that happens, its members would be so eager and can't wait for the next Sunday!

How Leaders Make It Possible

They pray, pray, and pray in their preparation waiting on God for directions pertaining to worship. Those on the podium should be conscious of what they are doing. They need to read these last three chapters on worship! No matter what their roles are, they are participating in priestly ministry. As visible and audible leaders, they are prompting their congregations to follow the Holy Spirit in them, and they point them toward God through Christ in unity. They are directors of a drama meant to ascribe honor and glory to the loving and almighty God. They represent the people in a special way to call on God in a Christ-like manner and represent them at God's right hand. He presents Himself to the people through the worship leaders.

Leaders in worship (not just the song leaders)occupy a very important place; they help others make it or break it. They hold the key to the worship in that place by their groups of believers.

Teach the People to Worship by Leading Them

Though in theory, worship could occur without an earthly priest or leader, in today's reality, leaders have a lot of work to do. As discussed above, Christians are not naturally ready to worship due to various reasons—at least presently, but I hope for a better future. The people up front assume a great responsibility for helping the congregation come to God the right way. People need guidance, direction, education, and models of God-fearing, God-honored lives. They need caring and understanding leaders who like Jesus Christ serve as faithful priests between God and them. People need to be led to the throne.

Select the Leaders or Prompters

As church leaders and pastors of the church, we need to identify people in the congregation who can grasp these concepts and are ready for training as worship leaders. We should select people who are God-fearing, faithful, available, and teachable who will gladly assume the responsibility of leading people to worship. Many senior pastors have wished to do the worship leading alone and have overlooked the need for involving and training members of the congregation, but we can see from the above discussions that it is just impossible for them to do all the work particularly if they serve fair-sized churches.

Train the Leaders

Many churches have taken the above step but have failed to provide training for those involved or have failed to get them to attend the training. All may be well if those who lead are educated men and women who are constantly learning, but that is rarely the case. We must be committed to the ongoing process of learning to communicate, leading, and making discoveries about God's person and work of grace and wonder. People need to be continuously kept in touch with what God is doing in the church and be stimulated to reflect on what the people of the church are into. We as leaders must be sensitive to and know our people.

Labor to Achieve Good Planning and Preparation

Since worship deserves every bit of a congregation's energy, we cannot afford to run carelessly constructed programs. If we are handling a six-hundred-person worship service, each minute used in a one-hour service consumes six hundred person-hours. This should spur us to careful planning and programming as we realize we are using people's time and opportunity to come to God.

We need to order our programs so there is a meaningful continuity between them. We need to anticipate the pathway and mark the milestones the congregation goes through emotionally and spiritually through each act of worship. We need to discover and learn to describe where we are and visualize and describe where we want to lead the people.

Planning worship is like planning a vacation. It involves careful planning for the use of time and creativity in providing situations that foster the excitement and encounters outlined above in some of the key activities in the program. We measure people's movement in a number of seconds; we prepare for what is said by thinking things through, writing it down, praying over it, and revising it according to God's guidance.

We should put great effort into preparing our sermons so they become God's words, not ours. Likewise, choirs should labor to give God the best in all aspects of their preparation and performance. We celebrate God's grace and love and manifold blessings He has bestowed on us. When we learn He deserves our best, we are happy to give it to Him.

Be Open to and Depend on the Holy Spirit

Many churches tend to work out things by their own training, planning, and power without leaving room for the expectations or awareness of the Holy Spirit's work.

Tradition is good, and heritage is important, but we must not hold tradition and heritage higher than we do God's truth. Since we are so much better educated today and are a new generation with access to the vast body of knowledge and opportunity to form our own balanced views, let us come before the Lord in spirit and truth. Let us leave behind the pretense and bondage of man-made rules, which we once unknowingly but willingly submitted to but now realize contrast with God's glory. Let us hold God's praise and glory more valuable than our personal and even denominational dignity. We should consider what David did while celebrating the return of the ark of the covenant. Let us come together in unity under the guidance of God's Word and the Holy Spirit and let it happen.

Conclusion

Worship is indeed a lost jewel of the evangelical churches. It is also God's lost jewel. For God's glory and honor, for the meaning of existence and purpose of the church God called and created in Christ, this missing jewel must be recovered soon. We can do a lot to help bring this about.

The discussion in this book is by no means all inclusive, but I hope that the trend of thinking can be understood and applied carefully, prayerfully, and with spiritual wisdom.

Let us not be idle and complacent of the status quo. We must break into glory! Let us be diligent in working with all we have to recover this precious jewel for God and the people He has placed around us. May we glorify God in our work!

CHAPTER 8

Worshipping through Stewardship

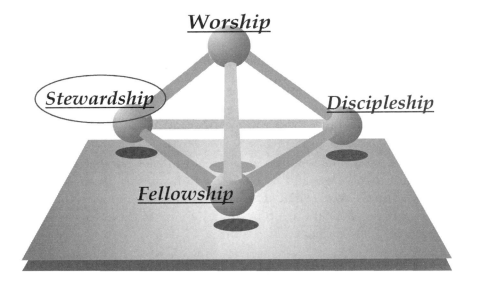

Worship

Stewardship

Discipleship

Fellowship

Introduction

We have touched briefly on the fourth commandment concerning the sabbatical rest. It must be clarified again that the rest prescribed in the fourth commandment is not a private rest, that individuals becomes the sole owners of the day, that they can spend it however they like. The traditional interpretation of the command to keep the Sabbath focused only on resting. To some extent, it has led God's people to lean on the day of rest and in many cases not to miss the meeting for worship.

The traditional interpretation may have missed two important things. First, it is not just a matter of resting for recuperation; it is to be a ceremonial rest to the Lord. Taking the day of rest to do only what one privately wants is a shortsighted interpretation and application of this command. Many North American communities, however, emphasize Sabbath keeping as taking the day off to enjoy hobbies, golf, soccer, TV, and so on. We are to take the day off and assemble in God's name for His purpose so we will be reminded of His lordship. Sabbatical rest must follow God's instructions. True Sabbath is an act done toward God. Doing rest is a thing to be done, just like the usual work need to be done. Faithfulness in carrying out the sabbatical process demonstrates our submission to God's lordship, trusting Him for provisions and our presenting ourselves as His stewards.

Many good theories have been written about rest, the Sabbath part of the fourth commandment, and I am not going to repeat what our dear brethren have said. Let us turn to the second part of the fourth commandment, which is about work. Clearly, our theological interpretation of the fourth commandment consists of not only the instruction to keep the sabbatical rest but also about the responsibilities God has entrusted us with and even ordained for us. This is a very important complement to our common understanding of this commandment.

In a previous chapter, I pointed out at some length that we are to work hard for six days and then take the Sabbath. In this chapter, we will focus on the second half of the commandment. A gracious agenda and a privileged relationship are quietly embedded in this—God's passionate desire for our stewardship.

Common Concepts of Work and Rest

The concepts of work and rest vary so much among different people. Differences may exist between Christian and non-Christian, those in America and those in Angola, people in Canada and people in China. Some people work to get the basics for survival, others work for fulfillment, for amass wealth, security, enjoy the good things in life and some for actualization, others work to serve the world, and still others see work as an unavoidable evil that interrupts the fun of life.

On the rest side, some people rest for the sake of work, some just enjoy rest and try to rest all the time and want to do as little work as possible.

There may be more views than the above concerning work and

rest. Is there a comprehensive foundation that encompasses and give meaning to work and rest? I believe the answer is in a principle of stewardship based on the fourth commandment. Let us examine some of these views and point the way toward taking work and rest in light of God's will.

Slavery to Survival

Only a small and fortunate bunch has survived to retirement and has made it all they dreamed for. They have balanced material possessions, health, and relationships. But most of us focus on the connection between work and survival. Human work is a part of the dynamics of God's living and unfolding creation. Not-yet Christians and some Christians alike work long hours thinking if they worked any less, they might lose their competitiveness or worse, their jobs. Parents teach their children that they should see studying hard as a good virtue or habit so they can survive in the highly competitive job market and economy. From all sides, we are led and in many cases forced to work hard. No one will help us if we do not help ourselves. Many people are enslaved under this invisible yoke of work. They have come to accept this as a hard fact of life.

Some people in developed countries have blessed educational opportunities and resources; they hope for success and aspire to become what the world recognizes as self-made people. The less fortunate keep grinding at the mill and never ask themselves, *"What am I working so hard for?"* because they thought they already know the unfortunate answer. They only wonder, *Is there a way out?* Worse, some break down under the yoke and lose their minds, health, sense of self, and hope. They spend the wealth they worked so hard for on maintaining their marginal health instead of on their dream retirement lives they thought they were working for.

We will never know how many people are living marginally and barely surviving. Too many people are enslaved willingly or not, but they are oblivious of to whom they are enslaved. Those brave enough to examine the reasons for their labor will discover they are following a dream that society has sold them on like the American Dream, which might as well be called a material dream. This is a vicious cycle fueled by the greed of businesses and the desire for material things on the part of the consumer-dreamers.

For some people, if they get a day off at all, they would try to work on that day to make up for what they have failed to do or recuperate before another crushing week is upon them. People who treat work as a survival necessity know of no way out. Survival or surviving well materially might often be seen as the objective of being alive and even the meaning of life. They go in and out each day taking only as much rest as they need for the next day's work. Some may have occasional entertainment or physical exercise but keep these luxuries under control so there is enough energy for the next day's work. Some even get by on only work, eating, and sleeping for months and even years until they collapse under the load.

Some who live in such a fast lane do not actually survive. All that pursuit in their younger days becomes just an empty dream as they are forces to offer whatever they have to the medical and health care professionals. What then could be the meaning of all that toil for survival? Was it for funding doctors and medical research?

How many survived well and those who didn't end up in death? Towards the end, those who made it realize that their material dreams die along with all those who only craved it. Some have nothing to let go of, and others have let go reluctantly of all their wealth. One way or the other, we know there is still something missing in the meaning of the daily survival toil.

Slavery to the Judgment of the Fall

I once believed that hard work was the result of God's punishment for Adam's and Eve's sin. One day, I was on a bus going to work because my car was in the shop. The sun was shining, and the bus ride was great. I was reading a book and thanking God for such a nice day. I wished I could skip work and just enjoy the day. Well, I still had to go to work even though my job was at a Christian charity. I just had to accept it and live under that curse. Work became harder for me because I was not motivated and it meant no more than inheriting another's punishment. My only hope for relief was the completion of my life on earth. That became a heavy, enslaving burden on my heart. I wonder how many of us hold this view at one time or another. By God's grace, soon after I had such thoughts, my pastor preached on this subject and changed my view. The sermon was about the biblical view of work. I will save the important teaching for later discussion, but for now, let me just say that work is not the curse of the fall though the judgment of the fall made work harder. Work was there before Adam and Eve were created.

God, Help Me to Do Well

Leaving the not-yet Christian's view aside, I want to trace some other viewpoints of work among Christians. Christians are different from those who fend for themselves without help because they have God on their side. For some of them, work is a necessity of life. They need to survive and do well. There are many challenges in the work itself, and then there are social and work challenges. These Christians pray that God will come to their rescue. They pray for the needed idea, solutions, promotions, and business outcomes. They pray that people will treat them fairly and kindly. They pray that they will not fall victim to their office politics. We all like to enjoy a steadiness and progress in our careers. After all, isn't it a good testimony for God if we, His people, do well in our careers? That proves God's reality and presence and demonstrates that He takes care of His people. In the 1970s, we were first taught this concept as students and members of churches.

A Higher Vantage Point

However, it is more than our doing well for His glory. As I mentioned, the sermon on work my pastor preached pointed out that we were made to work even before we existed. God wanted to create man "and let them rule over ..." A management job was prepared and prescribed for humanity even at the design stage. Work is ordained and sacred. Work is not the result of the fall. Thus, along with the responsibility to work, we are given the ability to accomplish the work.

Apart from the curse pronounced in the judgment immediately after the fall, proper work was never condemned but rather approved and rewarded. The Old Testament records how God blessed the work of the faithful, diligent, and trusting. Diligence at work is even taught in Proverbs. In John 5:17, Jesus declared with no need for context but as a matter of principle that the Father had been at work all the time and that He was still at work. In his letter to the Thessalonians, the apostle Paul pointed out the need for proper work for those who misunderstood the time of Christ's return. He forbade those who refused to work to partake in the communion meals as that put unnecessary burdens on those who supplied the provisions by their diligent work.

Yes, the whole work concept is rooted in the Creator. There was no concept of human beings before His design, and there was no purpose for being human until God had that idea of extending His nature, ability, and delight in working. We were created to work just as God works. When God came up with the idea of creating us and giving us His image, He blessed us with a portion of His working nature. Work is a part of human being and being human. God works, and in His image, we work. We were created as working beings like Him but with limitations God set. He does not get tired and does not forget, but He built into human beings limits on their stamina, focus, and memory. After a while, we get tired and must stop for rest and recuperation. After some time, we forget and thus need to remember and refocus. God's wonderful idea was to build in us these limitations so we would at times need to stop. While resting, we would remember to spend time with our Creator. In Exodus 20, God gave the clear decree on the Sabbath, which keeps the Master-steward relationship clear.

Work for us has a meaning much deeper than just survival or to get rich; it is participation in God's nature. As we work in the world He created, a dynamic functional beauty unfolds and adds beauty to the existing world as it has never been. When we manage the earth, a harmonious working world becomes alive that could not have been if we had not participated in it. A society with a culture and possibly a variety of cultures may exist because of our participation in God's dynamic creation.

God is not only the one ordained the work necessary to provide for our needs but is also the source of all the responsibilities in our lives. God's creation is not a static, once-completed-ever-completed one. Our work is an integral part of that ongoing creation. The formation of community needs everyone to work a cooperative part to establish a fair and just economy that reflects God's character. This mission calls for efforts to uphold justice through wisdom, creativity, and faith. As those who give leadership to cities and countries know especially, these are no small challenges; they are hard work. Bearing, raising, and teaching children to follow God is another sacred but not easy responsibility God gave us. And managing the resources of earth we were to rule over (Genesis 1:26) has become a prominent concern during the last few decades as never before.

Therefore, work is not a human invention evolved from unknown factors nor came about as punishment because of the fall. God is the originator of all work and responsibilities. However, the hard work that came after the fall caused human hearts to bend. In their hard work, humans thought they needed to survive by the work of their hands. In that process, they forgot even in their hard work God was still the real provider behind the harvest. Because of this, He gave us the commandment of rest to observe that special Sabbath—a rest to the Lord. In this rest and the called assembly, His people are to remember His role as their Lord and provider. They are to exercise their faith during the entire week, trust God, and stay close to Him as they alternate between laboring and assembling before God. Properly working and resting humans are an integral and beautiful part of the God-created world.

This perspective is extremely important because it affects our hearts' journeys as we fulfill our responsibilities and then rest. Those for whom the Lord is not lord, boss, or caregiver must try to create their own sense of security. If they realize the Lord rewards the efforts of those who trust and rest in Him, they will learn that their security is with the Lord. They will also know that along with their work, their sabbatical rest and their diligence are acceptable worship of the Lord. They will enjoy the security of God's provision and pleasure with them for being under His lordship. They will come to see themselves as servants of God rather than only laborers for themselves. For the gracious lordship of God over them, they will gladly accept and fulfill their responsibilities and do their best in their work truly as to the Lord. With that in mind, let us explore the application of the important discipline of work under God's lordship - stewardship.

Something happens in heaven when God sees people working diligently and according to His design and will, especially if they work to offer Him their faithfulness in stewardship. There is an active relationship between them and God through work.

The value of our work then goes beyond service on earth. Something beyond the earthly economy happens that links earth and heaven, God and us, in the spiritual realm. It happens between hearts, between our spirits and the Master's Spirit, between servants and their Master. God searches for such hearts for His honor's sake and will count such spiritual service as worship.[32]

Transformation through Stewardship

Those who learned to work and live lives of stewardship to the Lord at an early age may use the same attitude of stewardship all their lives. However, most of us need to make this important inner transformation

---

[32] Romans 12:1–3.

to enrich the routine things we do daily with this spiritual dimension. Let us consider the excitement such transformation can bring as we walk through life from young to old.

Early Childhood and Adolescence

Let us start with the very young. Those who are led by their parents have only a limited awareness of choice. Once children become aware of their roles in decision making on any decision, they can learn stewardship. Children's responsibilities increase over time and include those they receive not only from their parents but also from their teachers and other authority figures including the Lord.

A common thing for parents to do—if they do anything at all—is to tell their children, "Let's put you toys away." Some will say, "We're tidying up so the room will be neat and clean." They could seize such an opportunity to foster their children's becoming stewards of the Lord by saying, "God wants us to be tidy. He is pleased when we tidy up." This instruction conveys not only that there is an authority higher than the parents but also that the parents honor God's lordship and character of tidiness. We should never underestimate the power of such simple teachings. In this way, parents exercise stewardship over their responsibility to train their children. Especially if both parents have the same attitude, they teach their children about the ultimate authority in the household—God.

Imagine if parents used this approach to teach their children every new responsibility. What joy it is to see children realizing that their growing up plays a part in becoming young people for God and His well-organized world. What joy it is for us to see on top of having tidy rooms, children learning good manners as being accountable to God! And good grooming, recreation, health, chores, and education work that each and all responsibilities are all for God! Imagine how much we would honor God and bless our households if we trained children this way.

There may not appear to be any difference in the actual activities of learning and doing things while applying the principle of Lord-centered stewardship. The difference is in the inner being, the emotions, and the new spiritual engagement. In the beginning, spiritual awareness will indeed be awkward and unnatural, but in time, the habit of being spiritually alive will become second nature.

Transforming children toward godly stewards is the process of instilling and nurturing God's lordship in their lives so a spiritual dimension will be active at all times. They will automatically seek God's seal of approval on everything they do. They will engage with the people and things around him and by faith with God. They will rise above their physical and social dimensions and well-seasoned in the spiritual dimension when they fulfill their responsibilities.

Parents must be careful not to impose their own ideas or ways in the name of the Lord because young minds are clear and will one day discover the selfishness or falsehood of their parents. This not only places the parents' authority over God but can also damage the children, the parent-child relationship, the God-child relationship, and the child's faith and development. Helping a child transform toward God-centered stewardship certainly involves the parents' faith and discipline as well as the discernment of God's will.

God's blessings will follow throughout their developmental days when these young men and women train themselves further in their stewardship as they enter high school and college. These young people will unlikely to fail their school work or any responsibilities, as we see being too common among young people. By the grace of God, they may instead be much more likely to find success in their careers and relationships. Above all, the most important value of this is God's pleasure and honor as their Lord and the blessings He is so willing and eager to bestow.

Early Adulthood

Adolescent Christians move into a stage of life that brings new challenges and responsibilities. Their peers, the media, and their spiritual leaders take over the influence of their schools and parents. Young Christian men and women who were not set on a course of stewardship earlier should make the turn to become God's servants. Many will go off to high schools, college and take responsibility for their majors, careers, and friends. They must also begin managing their own rooms and purchases including necessities and entertainment. It is precisely in these new areas of responsibility that they can adopt God-honoring stewardship.

Young people often make decisions based on peer pressure, instinct, media, advertisements, and beliefs. Though people may say that they are making independent decisions, the habit of following someone else or some value system has often become so natural that they do not notice it. Their so-called independence could mean only an independence from their parents, following some unknown new masters.

Making the turn to God-centered stewardship means they will learn to reorganize that value system. They need the same basic truth mentioned before about their participation in being completed in creation – continuing God's unfinished creation in their own persons. Then, instead of simply following their instincts, the opinions of their friends, and values suggested by the media, young men and women can stay open to and submitted under the Holy Spirit. Healthy Bible study, steady devotional life, Bible reading, and godly fellowships are thus very important for young people so their minds and hearts will be prepared for such reflection. It may be awkward in the beginning to analyze what is going on in their minds, but this step is important so that young people will become aware of whom or what they are following. They will need to make conscious choices and engage the Holy Spirit as they make their decisions and carry out their actions.

The God-centered stewardship mentality will cause a phenomenon in the performance of our young men and young women just as what we saw in Joseph and Daniel in the Old Testament. God is so willing to bless their lives that their success will be exceptional and clearly demonstrate God is on their side. God gives blessings to demonstrate His presence, approval, and seriousness with people who trust, love, and serve Him. This is one of the most effective ways to draw other young people to God. Those who witness the process will be impressed and open up to God and the message His faithful stewards share just as what we see in Joseph who was sold to Egypt by his brothers.

In Business, Careers, and Homemaking

Some are further on in life in careers, in business, or in being homemakers. Likewise, adults in the busiest season of their lives need to discharge their many responsibilities to the Lord in addition to those people they serve. Christians should not simply pray that God will help them to do well in this or that; that exhibits a very self-centered and low view of their work and responsibilities. If they had been building their lives based on the worldly philosophy of success, survival, and getting ahead, we must make the transformation. They should learn that they were placed in their vocations to perform sacred work in the world God is continually creating. Their work is holy. They must learn to see deeper in what they do at work, home, church, society, and as world citizens fulfilling God-ordained responsibilities in their stages of life.

Our thoughts are active even if we do not know it. We have fears, debates, and reasoning every time we struggle at work. The value systems come up every time so we can establish the path we need to take. Transformation toward God-centered stewardship requires us to make God's lordship the priority all the time. We can also enjoy the peace that comes from knowing God is there taking care of us as His servants and is pleased when we serve Him through our careers. We are no longer fighting the battle for or by ourselves.

The meals homemakers prepare will be so much richer with heart for their families and God when they prepare them as servants of God. For the artists, the creativity of pieces of art will be so much richer when artists are walking spiritually with the master Creator. Business deals will be blessed, and problems solved as business people work for the Lord rather than just profits through these opportunities.

God's servants will be strongly motivated in their careers to balance advancement, health, family, social responsibilities, and living in an environmentally friendly way. This is because they will do everything under the lordship of God and for Him. Life at the career stage will no longer be wasted to slavery under the cold Massa[33] economy. The norms for God's servants at work will be productivity, a good work ethic, diligence, a cooperative spirit, a willingness to learn, willing to take on extra responsibilities, balance and God's special presence.

In Public Office

Christians with careers in government should become the best officers and civil servants because they are certain by faith that they are in office for the Lord as His servants (Romans 13:1). I am especially touched by the comment of the Hong Kong Special Administrative Region government CEO who upon taking office said, "I will do my best on this job." I think he would possibly share the same attitude as one of those godly government leaders. Christians in all ranks of public office should take that same attitude—that they are representing not only earthly government but also heavenly authority. Avoiding bribery and being upright, objective, kind, helpful, and service-oriented along

---

[33] Massa means: the Master. It was used by black slaves in the days of slavery.

with all the good qualities desired by the public would be the basic requirements, and typical of God's servant-stewards in government.

I speak of government offices separately because public office is an especially challenging place due to its accountability to the public. While most democratic free countries allow freedom of speech and criticism even against governing officers and parties, these free countries are in reality in constant political battles among the different political parties. Opinions and criticism from both the public and opposition parties are constantly distracting in such offices. In countries that discourage criticism against the governing authorities, constructive opinions and criticisms can only be deliberately gleaned from the people or from hearing God's prompting. In either system, God's stewards will not be deaf to criticism and suggestions, but they can seek God's guidance of God as a more powerful influence. Policies should be fair, just, and for the good of the people independent of the type of government. Governments can be transformed if more and more officers will take on a God-centered heart for service and stewardship. This transformation can happen in both democratic governments and single-party autocratic governments and God will be pleased with these officers in either case (Romans 12:8). People will value them, and God will bless them. They will be satisfied in their jobs because they will know the eternal value of what they do, and they will rest assured they performed a good service for God and others.

In Retirement

The concept of retirement changes as this social system evolves along with changes in health and the nature of the workplace. Many look forward to comfortable materialistic focused retirements in the last few decades, but most of the world has no such privilege. However, it does not matter if we made it or not; there is no retirement from God. We are to fulfill our responsibilities as long as we live. Thus, career-retired Christians still need to adopt the attitude of God's servants. They must not view their lives for enjoyment only and as an entitlement; they must understand that God has entrusted them with their resources not only to be enjoyed as He allows but also for His purpose.

Christians who retire from a career means that their stewardship of more time and resources can still be available to things other than career. Stewardship does not change after retirement. Christian retirees should become as active as they can be and be involved in

God's mission locally and globally. Mentoring, giving advices from their experiences, coaching, listening, giving care are things many retirees can do to serve their successors and to their peers. They should serve Him not because they want to show off their experience and the old way; they should instead be humble, teachable, and flexible. As long as we have breath, we are servants of God, and there will be things we can do in ministry or in the community. The stewardship mindset can give a beautiful transformation to Christian retirees allowing them to have yet another level of life satisfaction and opportunities to walk with God bringing Him honor.

The Sabbath

People at every stage of life can be servant-stewards for the Lord. We must learn to be aware of this important part of stewardship. Sabbath is the day of rest shared by all. In the sabbatical assembly as we worship together and remember the Lord, we will have much fruits of stewardship to offer in our prayers. We should all come before the Lord in prayer and ask Him to accept our work as worship of Him. This will greatly enrich our weekly worship in church.

Worship by faithful stewardship

Imagine a society in which people are consistently fulfilling their duties and responsibilities! I think the country would be so different as would our society. The companies these people work for would be different. These people would be actualizing God's will on earth and bringing blessings to their generation.

But those would be the only benefits on earth. What happens in heaven when more and more people in our congregation are fulfilling their school, work, home, and community responsibilities as stewards of the Lord? There will be joy in heaven. The Lord listens attentively to their prayers and accepts their love and respect.

If we have been teaching and training our congregants to fulfill their work with this stewardship attitude, we would have cultivated one important aspect of people's lives for God. Our efforts of pastoring have yielded good and lasting fruit for God and His kingdom. Our collective stewardship would then truly be our practical worship all seven days of the week!

CHAPTER 9

Worshipping through Fellowship

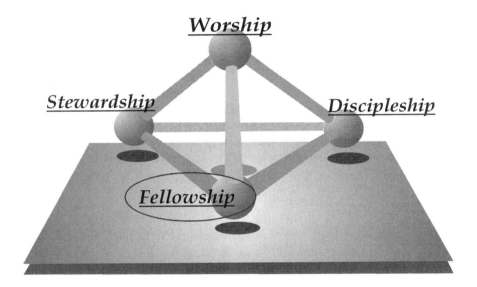

In previous chapters, we explored a life of pleasing God by doing His will. We rejoice in the knowledge that God created, called, and redeemed us to worship Him. We have also discovered how we can transform our otherwise mundane daily responsibilities from just things we need to do into God-pleasing stewardship opportunities. Let us continue our journey of spiritual reformation with some insights into God's will through fellowship.

How do we usually learn about fellowship?

Through Experience

In the fellowship hall, a self-serve lunch was in process, and many members of the congregation were engaged in pleasant conversation. The groups were defined by hobbies (those with shared interests), by genders (women with women), and stages of life (students with students). Some were fellowshipping over the way the food was prepared, some were fellowshipping over ... Wait a minute. Maybe that's only gossiping! Some were trying to win a point here or there though there was no issue or argument, like every other time they conversed and talked as if they were characters in a soap opera. Others were sharing serious things and lending ears and hearts to each other. This is the common fellowship many North American churches are familiar with.

It has been very different in Chinese churches as they mostly have groups segregated by age or stages of life. These groups are called fellowships. New people are typically invited to churches as faith seekers brought into these groups by Christian friends. Concepts of church and fellowship are usually formed through the experience of the initial contacts and journey. There is usually no deliberate explanation of what church and fellowship are all about. Popular activities that happen fellowship are Bible study or speakers on special topics such as family relationships, or potlucks, outings, and sports. Everyone interprets these activities and forms his or her own concept of fellowship or of church. In Chinese churches, fellowship is seen more as a noun—the kind of meeting we attend—rather than as a verb—something we do—whereas in any other church I visited, these groups are just called groups or small groups.

What is fellowship? If these different clusters were fellowshipping, which among these fellowships would God count as good fellowship? I have stated above that fellowship is related to the last six commandments. What is God's will about fellowship reflected in these commandments? Let us see more real-life action in another setting. Maybe you have had this experience too.

It was about my own experience. I was really mad! I feared that if I continued arguing with my wife, I might lose control and hurt her. I decided to go outside and vent since I did not know what else to do. Having no one around to speak to, I grumbled for a while before turning to God. I complained to Him about how my wife had behaved and recounted all her wrongs. Then, the still, small voice came. Without commenting on my wife's behavior, God challenged me.

"Can you not forgive her?" God asked me.

"What?" I asked.

The moment was tense. God was silent and was seemingly waiting for me to bend. He seemed to be smiling too knowing that I would yield. Thoughts ran through my mind not about my wife's wrongs but about all the wrongs I had committed before God and some even against my wife. God brought to my attention that He would forgive me my wrongs as I forgave those who wronged me, and He had actually forgiven many of my past sins. You know what line in the Lord's Prayer flashed through my mind and heart.

A strange power came into my heart, and my spirit yielded to the Lord's way as I chuckled with joy. I was still a little mad and weak in my forgiving act, but my anger mixed with uncontrollable, funny feelings. I could not hold back a smile as I entered the house and walked toward my wife. I did not even know if she would accept me, but I said, "I'm sorry. I was mad, but it's okay now. God wants me to be nice to you, and I could not object." I could not conceal my joy or my smile even though I felt embarrassed. God had made me equal with everyone, so I submitted to God and fellowshipped with my wife. "So in everything, do to others what you would have them do to you, for this sums up the Law and the Prophets." (Matthew 7:12)

We didn't need a twelve-step self-help course, a TV drama, or a worldly culture as an example to follow; it was just a matter of obeying God's command of fellowship. I am certain my obedience to His call to fellowship pleased Him.

Let's consider another instance when I was really mad. I had been an integral part of the original church-planting congregation in 1976. I was active as a lay leader in many areas of ministry before and was then an assistant pastor. In 1998, an issue arose between me and the senior pastor, and I was half-withdrawn; I hoped the deacons would step in to help. I thought, *I wasn't perfect or even any good, but they shouldn't have treated me like that!* To make a long story short, the church wrote me a letter in September 1999 and asked me to decide—stay till the year's end or leave immediately with pay till the year's end. The letter opened with these words: "We have consulted our lawyers ..." Yes, I was fired!

I was furious. *What? What had they done so far to help resolving the conflict?* No one needs to know the rest of the letter to comprehend my feelings. That was difficult. I thought I had contributed greatly to growing the church in the twenty-plus years I had been there from the original 50 in 1978 to 750 in 1999. I was hurt and mad. I contemplated picking a fight thinking that they deserved it. *Should I repeat the examples of how church leaders had fought valiantly for themselves, or should I turn to God's Word?*

God intervened right then and placed in the room someone I trusted; her presence helped me quiet down and let God soothe me. I thought, *I need to respect the deacons and the pastors here as God's servants however unwise they seem to be.* For God's name's sake, for the sake of the church's stability, and for the people's spiritual well-being, I decided, *No fight! Let God take me where He wants though I'll have to leave the hundreds of friends I have here and go minister somewhere else.*

My family suffered a great deal because of the incident. As everyone celebrated the smooth transition to Y2K on January 1, 2000, I was in the deepest dark valley of death[34]. But I was determined to serve God by offering such fellowship. I am certain God accepted my attitude of fellowship among His army. Again, there was no power struggle drama, which is all too common and disastrous— just God's commands and the principle of fellowship.

God imprinted this truth on my heart one time as I searched for a pictorial illustration for handling church conflicts. A picture flashed before me while I browsed through visual illustrations on a CD. It took only a split second for one picture to catch me and for God to explain to me what it meant. The picture showed four tanks rumbling in the field with barrels pointing in the same direction slightly to the right, antennas pointing up, and the four captains in the turrets with right hands raised. The tanks were stirring up a great deal of dust and producing clouds of exhaust. God hinted in my heart, *what would they do if they were hit from behind by friendly fire?* Instantly I knew. The captains would maintain their direction toward the battle, not turn around. They would be faithful to their call and fight only enemies. Poorly performing soldiers on their own side were not their enemies; they would not fight them. Their lifted hands and the raised antennas told me how connected these captains were with their commander. I understood that staying in prayer and listening to God is crucial when I am under fire and particularly when it is friendly fire. Good or bad, my senior pastor and deacons were still my fellow soldiers and I theirs. I realized God had used an ordeal for His good purpose and had taught

---

[34] In my depression, I actually planned to end my life in the following February but I thank God for His intervention.

me an important lesson about fellowship. "Everyone must submit himself to the governing authorities, for there is no authority except that which God has established. The authorities that exist have been established by God." (Romans 13:1) "Love does no harm to its neighbor. Therefore love is the fulfillment of the law." (Romans 13:10) "Accept him whose faith is weak, without passing judgment on disputable matters." (Romans 14:1) Submitting to the church administrative officers, keeping peace and not passing judgment on fellow team members were the way God wanted me to do.

Common Concepts of Fellowship

Most people are like me and did not learn the concept of fellowship from the Commandments. In my case, I started with an experience with church youth groups. People enjoy a network of relationships that give them support on common experiences and issues. These kinds of fellowships based on common interests provide companionship, support, opportunities for the exchange of experiences, and spiritual growth, and they even bring new people into the church.

The interactions that happen in these church activities might even be disqualified as the spiritual fellowship God desires. When people exchange stories unaware that they are only trying to win approval, they are in a self-concerned state. Such interactions can sometimes contain an uninterrupted bragging match among all who are involved, and no one is ready to give recognition to anyone else. The true nature of these conversations is the fellowship of the self-worshipping ring within which people demand each other to be their worshippers. Organized youth, men's, or women's groups may have good music and teaching. The essence of true fellowship, however, may be totally missing in such gatherings if everyone has self-centered attitudes or spirits without a sense of togetherness or comradeship. The experience of true fellowship may be flashing in and out at random if such churchy activities are not intentionally made to be caring, accepting, loving interactions. These experiences fail to teach us the fuller and deeper meaning and the excitement of fellowship as we should see in God's heart; whether they are unstructured such as gatherings in the fellowship hall or structured such as a youth group meeting. True learning of fellowship that pleases God can be found in the scriptures rather than our incidental experiences.

Creation and the Fellowship Command

The two stories above illustrate how anger brought me into a vulnerable situation with the potential that someone could get hurt. Jesus's teaching in Matthew 5:21–22 linked anger to murder. There are many approaches to fellowship or mutual love among God's people that are true with every other topic too. One approach is highlighting the benefits while another might highlight its necessity. These are all valid reasons that should motivate us to initiate love for our neighbors and make us aware of the goodness we can achieve when we fellowship. However, I want to show you yet a deeper motivation for fellowship that actualizes our human design and pleases God.

Though we hear a lot of teaching about fellowship based on the New Testament as commands and teachings by the apostles and the Lord Jesus, the phenomenon of fellowship is actually rooted in God's own Trinity character before creation. The capacity of fellowship was graciously bestowed to mankind after God's own image. The six commandments to live out fellowship were revealed to God's chosen people beginning in Exodus. The principle of fellowship given in Exodus was perfect from the first declaration and needed no revision. God created human beings in His image to have harmony and peaceful interaction with each other and be kind and loving among themselves. Harmonious and peaceful relationships are one of the beauties of God's nature. He designed and created for His pleasure and that of those who live it by His will. God enjoys seeing human beings interact lovingly and peacefully. When that happens, the comment "It is very good" will resound in heaven and reflect the same pleasure He had at the time of creation. This gives us a hint of why God is pleased to "forgive us our trespasses, as we have forgiven those who trespassed against us." The harmony of human relationships not only brings joy to God but also honor.

Learning to Fellowship—Starting in the Family

Animals know to feed, care for, and defend their young by God given instinct. God also designed human family structure and parents for cultivating love and peace. By this design, the best place for children to learn about love—receiving and giving—is with their parents. After their formative years, children begin to relate to the rest of humanity and apply the last five commandments of mutuality with fellow human beings.

I quote again: "So in everything, do to others what you would have them do to you, for this sums up the Law and the Prophets." (Matthew 7:12)

Murder along with anger and violence are clearly in contrast to being kind and loving toward one's neighbor. As we do not welcome it, so we should not be doing it. Committing adultery is clearly offensive to the other person and his or her spouse. As we do not want to be offended by others' adultery, we should respect others. So it is with the mutuality in the Commandments against stealing, giving false witness against our neighbors, and coveting their possessions.

The more-detailed regulatory demands in Exodus and Deuteronomy show how God wanted love and kindness to guide our behavior in all our relationships. Just to name few of them are the jubilee year when debts were forgiven and slaves were freed, helping a neighbor's cattle out of trouble, lending to a brother when you have the means, not taking a pledge (mortgage) from a brother, not charging interest to a brother, and many others. The wording in the regulations and explanation God gave demonstrates how He cares in detail for the welfare of everyone He created and especially His chosen people. Extending God's attitude of kindness and love toward each other is the key to understanding fellowship, the spirit of unselfishness. In that principle, we also find in the New Testament the command concerning forgiveness, acceptance, and caring for each other. All reflect the goodness of God's image He graciously granted us.

Jesus frequently taught the importance of respect and honor for individual well-being, not rights. When an expert of the law approached Jesus (Luke 10), their discussion turned from how eternal life could be inherited into a discussion of who one's neighbor was. The parable of the good Samaritan pointed out what the good chosen people should have done. Based on the Commandments kindness was the assumed common understanding. The point of the discussion is about him not being able to see that he has neighbors all around. God created us to be with others He created so there would be an endless, boundless presence of neighbors with whom we have varying degrees of relationship and opportunities to exercise fellowship for ongoing beauty in God's dynamic creation.

In the Sermon on the Mount, Christ re-endorsed the spirit of the commandment to love our neighbors as ourselves. When the time approached for Jesus to face death on the cross, we see clearly His desire for the disciples to love one another in His prayer, and in the new command He gave them in John 13:35. Don't you think He would be pleased if His people actually loved each other?

The apostles gave us many "each other" exhortations. The epistles of John, Peter, James, Jude, and Paul impart Christ's teaching to love one another. I wrote this not to convince but to cultivate the heart for these commandments. So, let us receive gladly the teaching and pledge our obedience to the Lord as we read some of these precious words again from the gospels and epistles.

> "Teacher, which is the greatest commandment in the Law?" Jesus replied: "'Love the Lord your God with all your heart and with all your soul and with all your mind.' This is the first and greatest commandment. And the second is like it: 'Love your neighbor as yourself.'" All the Law and the Prophets hang on these two commandments. (Matthew 22:36–22:40)

> ...I have not come to abolish *the Law or the Prophets*; . . . but to fulfill them ... You have heard that ... "Do not murder," ... But I tell you that anyone who is angry with his brother will be subject to judgment ... If you are offering your gift at the altar and there remember that your brother has something against you, leave your gift there in front of the altar. First go and be reconciled to your brother ... You have heard ... "Do not commit adultery." But I tell you that anyone who looks at a woman lustfully has already committed adultery with her in his heart ... Simply let your "Yes" be "Yes," and your "No," "No." (Matthew 5:17–48; emphasis added)

Jesus's words were based on these six commandments. Then He went on.

> Give to the one who asks you, and do not turn away ... You have heard that it was said, "*Love your neighbor* and hate your enemy." But I tell you: Love your enemies and pray for those who persecute you, that you may be sons of your Father in heaven ... If you love those who love you, what reward will you get? Are not even the tax collectors doing that? And if you greet only

your brothers, what are you doing more than others? Do not even pagans do that? Be perfect, therefore, as your heavenly Father is perfect. Therefore each of you must put off falsehood and speak truthfully to his neighbor ... "In your anger do not sin" ... He who has been stealing must steal no longer ... Do not let any unwholesome talk come out of your mouths, but only what is helpful for building others up according to their needs ... Get rid of all bitterness, rage and anger, brawling and slander, along with every form of malice. Be kind and compassionate to one another, forgiving each other, just as in Christ God forgave you. (Ephesians 4:25–4:32; Emphasis added)

If you have any encouragement from being united with Christ, if any comfort from his love, if any fellowship with the Spirit, if any tenderness and compassion, then make my joy complete by being like-minded, having the same love, being one in spirit and purpose. Do nothing out of selfish ambition or vain conceit, but in humility consider others better than yourselves. Each of you should look not only to your own interests, but also to the interests of others. Your attitude should be the same as that of Christ Jesus: Who, being in very nature God, did not consider equality with God something to be grasped, but made himself nothing, taking the very nature of a servant, being made in human likeness. And being found in appearance as a man, he humbled himself and became obedient to death—even death on a cross! (Philippians 2:1–2:8)

Please also read 1 Peter 2–3, 1 John 1:5–7, 4:7–12, and any other passage that comes to your mind and you will be blessed by the warmth with which God fills your heart concerning His will for Christians to love one another.

Deeper and Higher—Flying High with Fellowship

The last six Commandments laid out the bottom line for fellowship. We should not do any less. However, there are at least a few levels above which we should practice fellowship according to Christ's principle of loving-kindness. High flyers will practice active love and kindness compelled by the love of God. People who practice high-flying fellowship reach out to give love actively. They are far above the forbidden limits of harming anyone. Midlevel flyers are not as active as high flyers but tolerate and accept others. They are also willing to forgive others as do the high flyers, but they need more work. While not reaching out to do good fellowship, those at the midlevel are just as welcoming to others in the name of Christ. Those who are on the ground-hugging, lowest level are those who struggle to accept others and are on the borderline. They keep only the minimum standards of the last six commandments.

Of course, according to Jesus's words "Be perfect," He calls us to be high-flying Christians in our interactions with others. Please do not think it is easy to fellowship on the lowest level because even willingness to eat together at the fellowship hall is a challenge for some people. It is a good start to cultivate God-pleasing fellowship by sharing meals together.

Actualization of God's Own Creation

Being unselfishly kind and loving based on understanding God's fatherhood over us is a deeply spiritual act of fellowship. There is no shortage of these around us: unkindness or disrespect to parents, murder (or harboring anger), sexual misconduct, stealing, upsetting justice, and harboring thoughts about acquiring what does not belong to us. Whatever their causes, they are based on self-interest of people whose heart have drifted from God. Such behaviors do not reflect the image in the goodness of God. They turn the harmonious human community upside down and violate the intention of human creation.

Only when we behave as God meant us to will we bring the praise and joy of celebration in heaven: "It works—they are in loving harmony and reflecting the image we have invested in them." We should never underestimate the value of bringing joy and praise to God in heaven by loving one another. Being in loving harmony pleases God and is enjoyable to those who practice it. True fellowship is the actualization of God's great design and the self-actualization of being proper human beings. It reflects the glorious loving character of God. Those who are in it should first enjoy the assurance of God's approval even before enjoying the peace they live in. Imagine you can do something so simple to bring joy to God and others![35]

Transformation in Fellowship

Earlier in this chapter, I painted a dim picture of the interactions among people in church meetings at which fellowship may not happen as it should. The good news is that true fellowship can happen where it should and everywhere else without having to plan new programs or different meetings. Instead of an alternative program or ministry, it involves a reworking of the heart. We can apply a renewed attitude and spirit to existing programs. More importantly, the kind of true fellowship that needs to happen in our lives should not be limited to church activities. According to God's design, true fellowship should happen whenever we meet with others with the proper spirit of fellowship. It can be at home, school, work, play, and even when we are alone with people in our hearts and minds.

Most of us are not aware that our habits, attitudes, and philosophy are not inherited at birth, but are learned some time later in life. The influence factors in our learning process do not necessarily align with God's will or commands. Though we are not aware of these underlying factors most of the times, they subtly determine how we respond to others. The processes of formation may even be obscure most of the time. They will be noticeable only when we start deliberately to turn to God's way. We may need to learn these changes several times over before such mistakes start to diminish.

Again, the turn of the attitude, the shift in the spirit, and the follow through in actions will at first be awkward. Failure may even follow us for the rest of our lives. Yet the obedient heart and time will help us form new attitudes and habits. This new understanding of God's will and heart will change our attitude. I hope that the earlier part of this chapter has already helped launch you on this new journey.

Conflicts, disagreements, and differences are issues to be solved or resolved in the worldly mind. When considering the principle of fellowship, we can see these dark matters differently. We see them in the bigger picture as only the settings and challenges for maintaining

---

[35] Self-actualization is a common concept that the psychologist Abraham Maslow used to illustrate fulfillment. I do not have the right word apart from this concept to describe the highest sense of fulfillment regarding pleasing God, self, and neighbors.

and achieving fellowship and harmony to please God and others. They become the darker background on which the beautiful colors of fellowship can appear. Instead of dreading their presence and blaming others for bringing them to us as painful experiences, we can accept them so much more easily because we understand the spiritual battle between God and the devil. They are opportunities to work with each other on these problems so God will win and receives glory in the process of these spiritual battles.

As we understand that these hardships are God sent, we will wade through them with the assurance of His presence and approval as we do His will. Our joy and sense of fulfillment and security will increase. How exciting it is that after the first or second experience of such a journey, we will acquire joy in the face of difficulties and conflicts! We will become different persons bringing blessings even simply with our smiles.

Under the old way of thought, we may attend small groups and other fellowship meetings aimed at learning or receiving support or for another purpose. With the renewed insight into fellowship, however, we can enter a new dimension. The inner spiritual journey of our souls interacts with our minds with the intense presence of God. We know that He watches for the fruits of love, kindness, service, and the like as we walk with Him ready to bless and greet others in Christ's name. Our interactions in church meetings may have been rich in content, of high quality, informative, socially enjoyable, and spiritual, but the sense of comradeship increases twofold in this new spirit and attitude of fellowship.

These activities take on a new dimension and become a journey we take with God and those around us. Bible study, singing, sharing, listening, and even casual chatting take on new meanings with the spiritual fellowship dimension. We train our minds and spirits to become more automatic; and ultimately, we bring pleasure and blessings to people and glory and joy to our Father, Jesus Christ, and the Holy Spirit.

This kind of transformed spiritual fellowship will naturally bring further changes. We will want to do that more as we enjoy the fulfillment of giving godly love to others for reflecting God's image and giving God pleasure's sake. We will be living in and living out deep meaning and actualizing our lives as we go. This will motivate people to come out to meet up rather than being dragged out to meetings. Those who are not yet believers will be drawn to such a welcoming atmosphere and allow God and His disciples to minister to them. Good true godly fellowship advances evangelism.

This transformation to a deeper and truer fellowship also has implications for the fellowship ministries in our churches. Instead of evaluating the fellowship ministries based only on programming and operational elements and attendance, we should also observe to gauge the facial expressions specifically people's enthusiasm and joy, and listen to the interaction of people checking for godly relational loving words and body languages. Fellowship ministry organizers should produce programs that foster this new order. They will be relieved of the pressures of producing visible, bigger, and better stuff. Instead, they will be satisfied with following the Holy Spirit to create an environment for fellowship that will encourage attendees to exercise their freedom enjoying whatever teaching, interaction, study, food or chatting that might be there. The spirit of fellowship can also bear fruit even in Sunday school classes and the Sunday worship services. The renewal of fellowship lends great strength to churches that are struggling for meaning and vitality in their programs.

The renewed order of fellowship liberates those who are responsible for building loving relationships in the church from being constrained by the boundaries of interests and associations. People of different age groups, social classes, interests, backgrounds, races, and cultures can freely interact without the need for the usual common elements that bring people together. All they need is God's love in them and to know that the people in front of them are fellow human creations God loves; they don't have to be from the same denomination or even Christians. We approach everyone in and outside church with the attitude with which Christ would—we see them as our beloved neighbors.

All these new roads covered in fellowship renewal in a person cannot be possible if our *self* remains too much in the center. Just like iron cannot hold its solid state in the heart of the sun, the big cold *self* cannot hold back from melting down in worship where people encounter God. Then the warmed-up hearts become ready for real fellowship where honor is generously offered rather than demanded mutually. The gradually increasing sweet experiences of offering honor to others in harmonious relationship in the fellowshipping community will mark the way like new milestones of gladness. These milestones stay to testify to the joy of enjoyed fellowship and God's approval. Who wouldn't want to be in such a church?

So far, we have tried to envision these only in church settings, but these practices are not church-bound. Since the principle of fellowship is not a program or church strategy as we hear so much about these days. Rather, it is a principle based on God's heart in creation and command when He chose Israel. It is naturally applicable to all parts of life whenever people interact directly or indirectly. As in the case of my anger toward my wife described at the beginning of this chapter, we now understand why I could not keep back my joy as I did God's will. God intervened and healed the hurt in me as I chose to obey and follow God's way. The presence of God came into reality for me first and then to us as a couple. Isn't that beautiful? So it was, when I dealt with the struggle to fight back when I felt the church wronged me in firing me. I did not fight back and after that I was blessed, and the church was spared an ugly fight and God's name avoided another window of mockery. God won, the devil lost because of the Christian's obedience!

The renewed order of fellowship brings us back to the kind of society God commanded the chosen people in the desert to cultivate—a restoration to the original order of humanity that God created for Adam and Eve. This may be something fresh that you can apply to how you view your family members, coworkers, fellow students, business partners, bosses, customers, neighbors, and even the people you bump into at the supermarket. Note that all these relationships were important in God's heart as reflected in how they were discussed in detail in Exodus and Deuteronomy.

The requirements of Mosaic Law as well as New Testament teachings and commands reflect the same principle of fellowship—loving our neighbors as ourselves. Imagine no anger in your household after sunset. Imagine that no one will let seven years pass before everyone will let things go; and forgive even without the person knowing the offense or asking for forgiveness. Imagine being treated by others as though you were a precious, honorable child of the Most-High all the time. Imagine your spouse loving you not based on your merits but on his or her obedience to God. Imagine your parents accepting you regardless of your obedience or disobedience because of God's love. Imagine your children obeying you out of pure hearts because they know God's commands and promises. Imagine all this occurring not due to a legalistic motivation but because people are striving for self-actualization second and God's pleasure first. Imagine what a world that would be!

The beautiful picture painted in the last section may be unfamiliar, yet it is certainly not new. It is the original order of God's creation that once existed but was lost through the fall and the following generations who did not pay attention to God's heart. Many have studied the Bible only to miss the point. Now, you are one of the chosen to see this renewed vision of fellowship. The transformation of the new society begins at yet another warm spot, and you are given a blessed opportunity to be God's agent of change. Let's rejoice as we are in fellowship in the journey of pleasing God in this.

I have not covered everything I could have about renewal of fellowship, because I do not need to. I want to leave this as an open path so you may hear from the Holy Spirit yourself. The specific renewal will happen starting in your corner of the world.

Fellowship— Entering the Spiritual Dimension

The journey through this chapter has been a call to revive the spiritual dimension in our normal relationships. On the one hand, our relationship with God revives because of our awareness of His involvement in our being, specifically His creation and in His will for our daily relationships. On the other hand, there is revival of a spiritual dimension in our human relationships. On top of the social elements and factors, we now have a spiritual essence enriching all our relationships. With the added dimension of spiritual fellowship in relationships, people's satisfaction in relationships is fulfilled not only by the give and take of benefits or mutual interests. The derived spiritual values in the process relieve the stress of pursuing those socioeconomic expectations and open the door for spiritual blessings.

This makes a big difference in how we do meetings and intercessory prayers in church. The hearts of fellowship help to bring a new level of unity as we join our hearts in such a meeting. We can even feel the unity in our singing if singing happens in such meetings. The prayer items and requests are no longer the focus for repeated petition. How exactly has God answered our prayers would not the main objective that count for prayer meetings. God counts it precious as are willing to carry the burden of each other, seeking God for help and looking to Him in love and unity for our brothers and sisters. Prayer meetings may start with our interests in mind, but it will be God's interest in the end. He will thus likely listen intently and attentively and quite likely for His interest's sake, do the best in His will for us in response to our prayers.

Thus, we can approach Bible studies and classes with this added dimension and enrich church life. Even administrative and board meetings will benefit when we come with this renewed foundation of fellowship. The meetings will not be just about decisions or my way versus your way. Unity and the willingness to listen become core values as board members work together to achieve a living sacrifice to the Lord even before the final decision is made or the projects are carried out.

As mentioned before, this may be new to some of us, and many of us will need some time to get used to it. Rest assured that no matter how long it takes to experience the renewed order, you will someday find increasing fulfillment in your relationships. Relationship with those who were difficult will become cherished opportunities to serve God and others. You will become a better friend, parent, boss, client, business partner, and customer. You will be welcome in more places than before. Your social value will increase and even your commercial value may increase all by the grace of God, kick-started by your new knowledge about His heart for human relationships.

In time, the church will be full of fellowship high flyers because of God's love. They will actively extend love and reach out to make new, fulfilling, and productive relationships. Their sustaining hallmarks—kindness, welcoming faces and gestures, and joy in meeting people—will spread godly love in the community. The midlevel flyers will rise, open up, and accept people as they are. They will forgive others and become willing to enter deeper relationships as they should. They will be less inclined to engage in unnecessary arguments and do more listening and nodding than starting debates to show off their qualifications. They will be weaned off self-centeredness in time and improve their social and spiritual lives. Even the low flyers will want to rise from the dangers of offending God and neighbors. They will leave behind their habits of hatred, doing harm, succumbing to sexual temptations, lying, and stealing. Parents will be happier, and the young and adults alike will be kind and respectful to their parents whatever their ages.

I hope you will enjoy along with God the bright glory radiating through our loving fellowship with each other. Imagine what God will do when He sees His people doing His will in fellowship as we have envisioned it in this chapter. Imagine the joy in heaven and on earth when you offer to God daily the living sacrifice of fellowship in Christ's name according to His will and empowered by the Holy Spirit. May God be honored and praised for how we fellowship with each other! Will you offer your fellowship to God as a part of your worship?

CHAPTER 10

Worshipping through Discipleship

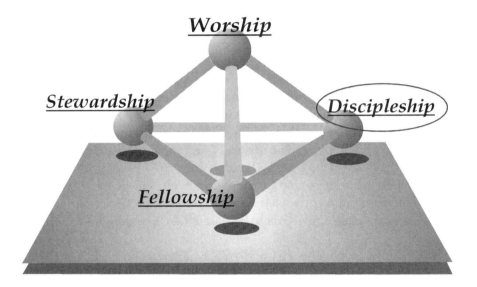

Worship

Stewardship　　　　*Discipleship*

Fellowship

Discipleship is a part of our worship

We have shown in chapter 4 based on Exodus 19–20 that the Ten Commandments and the Great Commission were the ways God wanted His people to live. We have also discussed briefly in chapters 5-9 the meaning of worship, stewardship, and fellowship based on that same premise. In this chapter, we will demonstrate that discipleship is the way God chose at creation and even throughout history to allow us personally to join Him in cultivating a people for Himself. Through discipleship we offer to God His desired people; that is in itself an act of worship. However, discipleship is a big topic that cannot be fully addressed in this short chapter. I have chosen to cover only the deep meaning and overarching objectives of discipleship to keep this chapter short. I will not address programmatic details such as small-group strategies, Bible study, ministry-skills apprenticeship, or other topics many other authors have handled well.

In chapter 4, I stated that the missions given to the Chosen People Israelites then and now the Church being the same based on Exodus 19:5-6, 1 Peter 2:9 as well as Matthew 28:19-20. This mission is discipleship - the fourth of our four ships. However, we should be aware that when the word *discipleship* is mentioned, people may actually have differing concepts popping out of their minds. Some focus on the process, program, or strategy while others think of the contents and skills propagated. Others think of the spiritual character and disciplines or spiritual practices, and yet others think of how to raise leaders to continue a church's traditional operation. Regardless, I invite you to leave your concepts behind and think in terms of the widest meaning of discipleship. In this book, the word *discipleship* is used to represent the missional concept collectively implied by the following three passages – to bring in and cultivate a people for God.

Now if you obey me fully and keep my covenant, then out of all nations you will be my treasured possession. Although the whole earth is mine, you will be for me a kingdom of priests and a holy nation. These are the words you are to speak to the Israelites. (Exodus 19:5-6)

But you are a chosen people, a royal priesthood, a holy nation, a people belonging to God, that you may declare the praises of him who called you out of darkness into his wonderful light. (1 Peter 2:9)

Therefore go and make disciples of all nations, baptizing them in the name of the Father and of the Son and of the Holy Spirit, and teaching them to obey everything I have commanded you. And surely I am with you always, to the very end of the age. (Matthew 28:19-20)

In Exodus 19:6, the chosen people were to display godliness in their lives and their religious rituals that would paint a picture of God's glory and honor. This should impress the Gentiles and help to convert them to worship and honor Jehovah as the supreme master of all things. Similarly, according to 1 Peter 2:9, Christians by their lives and messages should be the priestly agent that helped bring a change to nonbelievers' standing with God. By the very command of the Lord (Matthew 28:19–20) Christians should be going out to baptize people in the name of the Father, the Son and the Holy Spirit and teaching Christ's commandments. The Christians should declare and demonstrate God's goodness, holiness and justice. They should share the message of God's grace in salvation through Jesus Christ. These all should impress nonbelievers and cause them to turn from their ungodly ways and choose by their free will to accept God's saving grace in Christ and His Lordship. Discipleship is an interactive process of life transformation. It is also 'commissioned people in obedient action' bringing non-believers to God. By honoring and obeying the Great Commission call, Christians demonstrate by their action the Lordship of Christ. This submission is a form of worship especially when it is done in love, respect for God and glad obedience.

The Root of the discipleship concept

The word discipleship triggers a variety of thoughts in different historical and cultural contexts. It is important to note again that my use of the word here is rooted in the mission described by these three scripture passages, and not rooted in the etymological[36] studying the word. In these three passages along with the Ten Commandments, we see that God wants all people in the world to be blessed. Now again, God wants it firstly for restoring His honor and pleasure in worship, and secondly and as importantly for man for his salvation and the blessings intended for him from the beginning.

There is an increasing emphasis on Christian discipleship over the last five decades. My own exposure did not begin until forty years ago in the middle of 1970s. We studied Robert Coleman's book *The Master Plan of Evangelism,* Walter Henrichsen's *Disciples Are Made - Not Born* and a few others. Pastors and church leaders had proposed so many methods and wrote about principles concerning the best approaches to do discipleship. We have seen emphasis on using the

---

[36] I warn against a common danger of overgeneralizing theological terms by simply studying their etymology and allowing that to send us off on tangents. This is important not only to the theology of the word *disciple* but also for many other theological studies.

small group approach, using one-on-one approach, giving emphasis on Bible study methods, theology, creeds, character building, producing church ministry leaders. Everyone's theory has its own merit in its own perspectives! The latest and most popular of these in recent years are concerns of Life-influence-Life, and Intentional Discipleship and multiplication. All of these are wonderful. Yet, I think it helps to look at it in a fresh way by studying the root of discipleship in history.

Life-Influence-Life and Propagation

The life-influences-life concept has been receiving increasing attention ever since the 1980s. The phenomenon of one's life influence is neither new nor foreign to us at all. The nature of discipleship is very much about influencers (or masters) intentionally causing specific formations in the life of the influenced (disciples or followers). It often involves the propagation of skills, character and life-outlook of the master. Yet have you ever wondered where such a principle came from? Was there an origin for the effects of life influencing life?

Let us go back to the earliest point regarding the origin of humanity. In Genesis 1:26a, God planned the creation of man: "Let us make man in our image, in our likeness, and let them rule." God in His greatness and sufficiency did not need man to exist, but with pleasure He freely extended a part of Himself so a new kind of being would exist. If man were to exist for any purpose or meaning, it would be first for God and for His pleasure. Yet, we thank God as man was also blessed as God brought him into existence. God then created the necessary concepts of physical existence and the physical space. Man's blessed existence became possible and actualized by God's will and powerful word. As God breathed His Spirit into Adam, he became a blessed living spirit that resembled God to certain extent. This first man was formed reflecting a subset of God's nature. God was pleased and said, "It is very good" (Genesis 1:31).

Note that Adam possessed a nature that included intelligence, ability to listen and to speak, all by God's choice. He was formed receiving rulership, discernment, freedom of choice, the ability to express himself and more—right from God's nature. He was to also participate in further creation by God's command to be fruitful and multiply (Genesis 1:28).

Discipleship is a process of influence that propagates a nontangible substance. God was the first and primary source of the substance and influence. It is in God's own nature and was in His plan and He built it into humanity right from the beginning. He propagated it to the first man He created. Adam was the first one who received the substance. Ever since Adam's time exercising influence has been natural and automatic in everyone's life. As Adam lived with Eve and his children in the Garden of Eden, he would have caused an influence in Eve's and his children's lives.

We have a very natural tendency to share, teach, lead, and exert influence while open at times to receive influences even if we do not realize that. Everyone will give and receive in the life influence life process and concepts that dictate behavior are propagated along. Whether there is a program or not, a clear conscious intention or not, a strategy or not, life of a person will always influence those who are around him or her, and propagation happens. God desires an interacting human community to seek, cherish, and maintain the course in knowing and doing His will together by the process of influence, or discipleship.

The first instruction of multiplication was given to humanity – be fruitful and multiply (Genesis 1:28). Just as human beings multiply physically in the family, Life-Influence is a natural way to propagate or cultivate values and behaviors along the family and social structure. The way of how to relate properly with God can and should naturally be taught and caught in family and social settings. We see the illustration too that God wants His will to be maintained in our conversations in every setting of our lives (Deuteronomy 6:4-9).

So, discipleship was not a new concept that only originated in the Lord Jesus's Great Commission. The Lord used but a mechanism of mutual influence He built into man. It is His desire that man may by their free choice and by faith choose continually God's way again. Therefore, the emphasis in the Lord Jesus' Great Commission calling is not on intending to make disciples or not but should emphasize on the objective and results of discipleship. Disciple making for Christ is first to baptize people in the name of the Trinity and then teaching what the Lord had commanded (Matthew 28:19-20). The first part relates to the saving faith to become sanctified in Christ's name. The second part relates to learning the way of God-pleasing living, for righteousness' sake, for blessing's sake and most importantly for God's pleasures' sake. Discipleship involves both parts and not just one or the other.

What Fills the Mind Leads

God has not left us without intentional guidance regarding the ultimate principle of cultivating people for Himself. He created us in such a way that our actions follow what goes on in our minds. Some bad-influence game makers might deny it, but what fills the mind does influence a person's desire and eventually commits to action. I believe the most important principle concerning how to cultivate people for God is in Deuteronomy.

> Hear, O Israel: The LORD our God, the LORD is one. Love the LORD your God with all your heart and with all your soul and with all your strength. These commandments that I give you today are to be upon your hearts. Impress them on your children. Talk about them when you sit at home and when you walk along the road, when you lie down and when you get up. Tie them as symbols on your hands and bind them on your foreheads. Write them on the doorframes of your houses and on your gates. (Deuteronomy 6:4–9)

Using the Four Ships thought structure is a way to help us to keep God's Old and New Testament requirements in our hearts. We will keep think worship, stewardship, fellowship, and discipleship all day long. We will talk about God and His requirements all the time so that those we disciple will be flooded with God's will, and they will eventually choose holy paths at home and in school and work and be loving representatives of God. When that happens, we will not lose out in doing anything other people do in life except for sinful things. We will be sharing, accommodating, forgiving, and would be welcomed members of any community. We will be admired by all around us, and our words will point people to God. This is the fruitful culture God aches for, and that is what I want to offer God as a Christian leader.

I hope new and focused discipleship courses and materials will be produced based on the Four Ships thinking. I am convinced that it is what God wants in His people as this leads people to think of His requirements. But for now, the volumes and variety of programs and study materials may still be used effectively to cultivate people for God as long as we keep in mind the simple spiritual structure of the four ships.

Intentional Great Commission Discipleship

Discipleship is a process that teacher and disciple engage in together to transform the disciple's life according to God's objective. Its objective should not be reduced to just making church programs, Bible study, or the masters or teachers look good. The most dangerous kind and does most damage to God's kingdom is that leaders intend to collect disciples in the name of Christ but for their own personal agenda. Disciples' spiritual lives formed under whatever motivation would eventually multiply. That is why we must be careful even when we talk about intentionality in discipleship. We should mean we are intentional for God's purpose by God's way and not men. Since life-influencing-life is natural and automatic, discipleship processes can occur on a few levels and are different in their efficiencies and effectiveness. Let us examine them in a logical spectrum.

The most mild and inactive discipleship process is one which leaders would create an environment without pressure or intentional promotion. This kind of leadership allows disciples to discover God's goodness and will by themselves or the prompting of the Holy Spirit. They do not need to think much; instead, they can choose whatever they want to soak up offered by the activities and the atmosphere. Neither the teachers nor the disciples would necessarily care about causing God-pleasing life transformations. Disciples pick up what they see and usually do nothing deeper than scratch its surface, unless by God's grace.

The next degree of discipleship is when the teacher has a clear intention and the disciples accept the authority of the teachers, for example, pastors and want to submit to them. The disciples find pleasure to be with the teachers and would do as the figureheads say. They do not care for explanation or to understand the way or the reasons. In this kind of discipleship, there is very little, if at all, intention for the teacher to cause transformation of life in the disciples. The objective is perpetually having things done according to the teacher's way. Things can get organized and all kinds of meetings can take place. The disciples learn well to do ministries together promptly making the church look vibrant. This discipleship is really no different from any other organization at all. People join a church as their community, pay respect to the pastor or organizers, and learn to fit in. They participate in programs and may even help the leadership. This kind of discipleship is more community development; disciples are led and conditioned to join the operation without much need for spiritual formation or transformation. They just fall into line and seem to do well just looking as if they were in a spiritual environment and think they are being spiritual by getting involved. They feel no need to transform their lives to please God. I have witnessed this in many churches today.

The third kind of discipleship takes place due to the disciples' initiative, not the teachers' initiative. The disciples are hungry for growth and goodness. They may search inside their churches and possibly beyond and may come across something they appreciate. From appreciation comes a desire for imitation, and from imitation comes the internalization of a new quality. Life transformation can occur in these cases, but there is no certainty of what the disciples would become because the learner could have picked anything to learn and may miss God's requirements.

The effective discipleship process that may align more with God's desires is to cultivate a people for God by God's way. The discipler should be motivated by God's love for all mankind and be intentional not only for engaging the process but also for God's purpose. In this missional process of discipleship, teachers are motivated first by God's calling and transform lives for God; they grow disciples for Christ and send them on a God-pleasing journey as God-pleasing people. They offer God the fruit of discipleship, the Godward changes and formation that happen in their disciples' lives. God's call for His people to make disciples is more than soaking people in a church community and allowing them to become whatever turns out. Disciples must turn out to the kind of people God wants. Only this kind of discipleship can be acceptable to God.

Unfortunately, many church leaders are pressed by their ministry culture into busyness operating their churches. They spend most of their time to study for great-sounding technical or theological sermons or got sucked into church politics. As a result, they along with their team fail to realize the importance of giving adequate resources for intentional, life-transforming discipleship. This vicious cycle spirals out of control in many cases. Brothers and sisters, we must come back to heed God's call to foster intentional, life-transforming discipleship that is aligned with His love for the lost souls.

A clear purpose, intention and passion of loving the souls for God must be present for effective discipleship ministry. When these are largely in place (as we can never be perfect) effective discipleship can happen in many channels including classes, groups, sermons, books, or even social networks on the internet. Any gathering of two or more people can become an opportunity for discipleship. Wise leaders will choose the best channel for them in their contexts and not necessarily copy another church's or group's form and methods. Just as advertisements and salespeople do, they can sell anywhere people encounter them. We can make disciples anywhere too. Intentionality and passion will sustain times of hardship and distraction so we may bear abundant fruit in cultivating a people for God.

Direction and Vital Signs

As stated above, discipleship in general is a mutual process by which people influence others and are influenced by others. There is usually a balance of influences, except when things tip the scales and result in dynamic changes in peoples' hearts and behaviors. Political and commercial propagandas make use of this phenomenon daily tipping the balances to promote a product or a political entity. A similar spiritual dynamic is actually happening daily. Christians must realize that this spiritual warfare is going on between God and the devil, between good and evil. It is a tug-of-war between God's will to win everyone to heaven and the devil's desire to lead people to destruction. Which way would this tug-of-war shift or tip?

In reality everyone is following something in a mixed-up smorgasbord of influences. Even in churches, we find a mixture of subcultures that align with God's will and those off on a tangent and missing God's will. There was no shortage of such phenomena in Jesus's time. In fact, we started our search at one such juncture in Matthew 22:34–40. The Pharisees behaved according to some theology of their own and formed a distinct religious subculture. The Sadducees had theological beliefs that differed from those of the Pharisees'. The Essenes had another subculture and influence then. Each religious sect among the chosen people then was enticing people toward its camp intentionally and enthusiastically to make its own disciples. Even the apostles were initially part of that tension among the religious culture at that time before they met the Lord Jesus. When Jesus caught their attention by His power, miracles, authority, and graceful truth from God, their eyes opened and followed the Lord Jesus.

What these three religious sects experienced in Jesus's time might be exactly what we are experiencing today. I found so many directions in the churches I attended: One camp saw that the only thing that counts is true conversion. People are led from being non-Christian to converts to a saving faith in Christ. The goal of discipleship is a firm faith in salvation, but they do not much of what to do next beyond that. Another camp among those who call on the name of the Lord Jesus emphasize speaking in tongues and consider that a gift of the Spirit. Yet another camp emphasizes having biblical knowledge and the ability to quote scripture and demonstrate biblical interpretation. And there are still others emphasize enlisting converts into getting busy involved in church ministry. Church operations and institutional growth may become the ultimate objectives of some of these subcultures. They believe that once Christians are involved in church ministry, they will somehow find God's will and spiritually mature.

I do not need to list more examples as the sects we have today are even more complex than those during Jesus's time. It is time for our generation to desire an answer to this question: Lord, we are intentional with discipleship, but what is the central theme about discipleship among all those practices and theories passed down to us? I believe He would not tell us much more than what He told the Pharisees in Matthew 22:34 and He might even answer us in a similar way.

I am convinced that we should first come to the Father in Jesus's name. We should learn to love God with all we are and all we have, and we should love our neighbors as ourselves. The vital sign we should look for in God pleasing discipleship are rooted in God's Commandments and Commission. Are we making and multiplying disciples by baptizing them in the name of the Father, the Son, and the Holy Spirit and teach them He has commanded us to? Are we being fruitful in all seasons, bring glory to Him by making disciples that are after God's heart? What vital signs are your discipleship ministries showing? We should be looking for and check regularly the vital signs among the teachers and disciples in worship, stewardship, fellowship and discipleship in our discipleship ministries. Are these thoughts the prominent emphasis and are being propagated among the church?

The Fruit We Are Producing for God

I appreciate Robert Coleman's *Master Plan of Discipleship*, which triggered my first interest in discipleship. In the early 1980s, I was influenced by Pastor Yoonggi Cho's cell group concepts. A few other masters appeared along the way including some Chinese church discipleship champions. Eventually, I was exposed to Dr. Bob Logan's and Neil Cole's collaborative work *Raising Leaders for the Harvest* and Neil Cole's *Cultivating a Life for God*. These great contributions can help us develop well in the programmatic and ministry perspective. I could list many more here. I cannot outdo these masters and there is no need to repeat what they have so well done. They have brought so much to our generation. I am satisfied to bring just a new perspective so what they have taught may be even more effective and God pleasing in our inner spiritual journey.

There is no shortage of other programs, materials, study books, or strategies that promote discipleship. You may even have the same experience as I did when I searched Christian bookstores for programs. Choosing one gave me a sense of accomplishment but left me with the haunting feeling that I had passed up others good programs. All the training I had in exegetical preaching, Bible interpretation, small-group strategy, one-on-one discipleship, church history, and ministry skills seem like useful tools, but I found them aimless spiritually. I found that ministry skills themselves have no direct bearing in my relationship with God and what He wants. That was when I prayed as the pastor of Christian education and discipleship at a church and asked that same question the Pharisees asked, and I felt like a zealous Pharisee. The Lord answered by reminding me of what He had showed me in the summer of 1993 about the Four Ships concept. I started to understand what He was aching for—Four Ship Christians for Himself.

The Four Ships discipleship mind-set frees us from that haunting uncertainty of aimlessness. We realize whatever materials or programs we are using them for a clear purpose and a spiritual result. It is because of this that I stopped feeling guilty for not keeping all my church members in the Sunday school program to complete the study of the sixty-six books of the Bible in a long endless program. That kind of Bible book-after-book curriculum can easily take up fifty years of one's life and the main fruit of the system is a 'Sunday school curriculum' with not necessarily having a clear spiritual outcome.

"He has showed you, O man, what is good. And what does the LORD require of you? To act justly and to love mercy and to walk humbly with your God" (Micah 6:8).

Cultivating Four Ships qualities and daily practices fulfill the Lord's requirements for the chosen people and those in today's church. It gives God the kind of people He desires. The Lord led me to capture His heart in the years after that prayer at the bookstore. I realized that my job as a pastor was not to train scholars, seminary students, or workers for churches though we may as well have these. It was not just to evangelize and fill church and training programs with people. Nor was it to complete all the courses offered by so many publishers. My job was to cultivate a people for Him.

I am not saying that those curricula, strategies, programs, and courses are useless; I am saying that they are the tools and means to reach a goal—help people become what God wants them to become. We must never lose sight of that goal. I will find myself sinning and guilty before God if I lock people into all kinds of meetings and rob them of a fruitful and fulfilling walk with God.

One time, I met someone whose heart seemed to be on fire for the Lord. He had attended his church for a few years but wanted to do something because his church seemed too dead. There may have been a number of people in his church who wanted to change this dwindling church's situation. Everyone might have had a different answer to the question "What does God want from this church?" That question is always not only for this church but for all churches! I believe the Lord wants to repossess His people; He wants churches that will convert and produce people who understand what He wants; and live fruitful, fulfilled lives. Have your church programs been effective and efficient in producing people for God?

In many places in the world 90 percent of the population is outside of the church. Too many Christians feel comfortable because they themselves are in church but forget that God does love every soul who is outside of the churches. Many of these people will die without knowing God because the churches are not working fast enough to bring them into God's fold. New population will be brought in or born into the community and they too need to be brought into God's Kingdom through faith in Christ. We must make disciples at a rate that is much faster than the rate people are dying and born into the world. Even if every church in these communities can consistently bring in ten new converts for every one hundred of her congregation each year, keep every new convert in the church (or another church) and all have healthy discipleship programs at the same time; it is still hardly be fast enough to save everyone for God before too many perish without the gospel.

Yet how many churches have been producing this result in both evangelism and Christian discipleship? The Christian population percentage had increased so little or even declined for the last many decades for too many places. Don't we feel sorry because God is not getting His people fast enough before they die off?

We need a reformation, a deep change with a clear objective and effective use of all the good materials produced by our dear coworkers. We need to make the objective clear, and God's objective is not complicated. Intentionality is not to just have discipleship ministry but one that has that specific direction and results according to God's specifications. It really can be represented in this simple term: Four Ships people. A people who are trained to daily be:

1. God-honoring, God-Fearing, Happy, humble worshippers,
2. Faithful stewards for God who happily fulfill their duties and offer their labor to God as His servants,
3. Happy, fellowshipping loving people who make and maintain peace and harmony at home, work, and school, and in their communities, and
4. Disciples who seek after God's heart and influencers who guide others to Four Ships lives.

To put it even simpler: People who worship God by their Four-Ships.

My motivation for discipleship is no longer based on church growth, curricula, programs, or cleverly designed systems. I am motivated by only a few things all revolving around my love for God.

1. I want to address where He hurts—He lost His beloved masterpiece creation.
2. I want to give Him what He wants—God-pleasing, Four Ships people.
3. I want to give Him as many people as I can cultivate.

Our discipleship ministry should be an outflow of our relationship with the Lord. I do not expect in my discipleship ministry to yield many Bible scholars, apologists, pastors, or deacons for the local church, though some of my disciples might be by God's calling. But I expect people who will take the opportunities offered each day to live God-pleasing lives. Four Ships disciples will worship God, be good stewards, and be loving people and good influences wherever they are. They will constantly be in touch with God and offer their hearts and spiritual fruit for the Lord. They will evangelize and make disciples. They walk with God in unceasing prayer and are living sacrifices and blessings to Him and their communities.

Keeping the Main Thing the Main Thing

It is so difficult to keep the main thing the main thing today in our churches as the network of influences are discipling us in all directions. We have entered a crucial time when we need to come to the Lord for His answer. Christians everywhere have become like their mentors and teachers and exhibit the traits and characteristics of their masters. But do they know the essence of their spiritual lives? What values do you hold in your heart that God would consider passing on to your disciples? What does God want you to learn from your mentor? Are they in line with Jesus's answer given in Matthew 22:34–40? God's requirement for our lives is consistent throughout history; it was then, it is now, and it will always be. He will ultimately judge us all using the same standard.

The query for this central theme is what this book is about. We started with this question and found the answer in Jesus's answer to the Pharisees. We have further translated that answer and the Great Commission into the four ships—worship, stewardship, fellowship, and discipleship. That's what the Lord would require of us today and for the rest of our lives and for the lives of those who live after us.

Do we, our mentors, and disciples demonstrate these traits?

- God-centered worshipful life in attitude and practice
- God-centered faithful stewardship in all our responsibilities
- God-centered common love as the Father loves all humankind
- God-centered obedience in making disciples

Are we bringing people into God's kingdom through Jesus's name and training them to be good earthly and heavenly citizens by the help of the Four Ships concept to keep God's Commandments? Do we all exhibit the vital signs of authentic disciples and teachers? Are our mentors growing in these areas themselves? Are we passing on quality spiritual lives to others? If so, we are cultivating people for God.

There is nothing like a clear, simple, focused direction with a comprehensive 'product' description so clearly in accordance with God's Great Commission like the Four Ships culture. Discipleship is cultivating people for God so He can own and dearly embrace those who seek advancement in their worship, stewardship, fellowship, and discipleship.

I am excited to envision that clusters after clusters of people all over the world who are after God's heart. I see God smiling at them and wanting to bless them. I see how these people bless the world by their godly values and behavior. I see society blessed by their godly faithfulness in fulfilling their duties. I see people growing and blessed and extending their love to everyone else. The bright light of the Four Ships culture is a clear witness to God's presence among His people. Seekers are more likely to accept the testimonies and message from witnesses who exhibit this Four Ships culture.

Effective Great Commission discipleship must start with people who see God's way, learn and submit to His commands, practice it and demonstrate these spiritual vital signs. The passion of the Four Ships should be the DNA that dominates our ministries and signifies the true disciples of Christ.

Discipleship Occasions and Opportunities

Great Commission discipleship may happen anytime and anywhere in our lives. It can be done by intentionally organized meetings and it can also be done naturally without thinking if the influence giver is well practiced. As long as there is a passion of loving God and wanting to give God His desired people, it will happen and bear fruit. However, I just want to list out a number of church activities where we can build intentional programs for parts of the process. I will give a short comment about using music for discipleship at the end of this section.

a. Sunday school
b. Bible study groups
c. Discipleship study groups
d. Worshipping together, via sermons, songs, Scripture reading, etc.
e. Formal and casual fellowshipping with other Christians – meals, visitation, caring
f. Conferences, courses, seminary
g. One on one mentoring and/or coaching
h. Any time Christians may meet together face to face, over the network or through writing and reading, listening or observing one another. At work, at home and at play.

Each type of activities in the list above may be understood and used differently in different churches. It does not really matter as discipleship may happen whenever words spoken with the influence towards the Gospel or God's Commands in these settings. We just need to plan these activities with care so they will not become void of life-transformation towards God's desires. Again, the important thing is that there is a clear intention to use these activities to cultivate a people for God.

Much teaching materials have been published for Christians Education, Bible study and discipleship. Each author had designed his or her program with some purpose and objective in mind. There are just too many for us to even browse through and understand them. A piece of material may look good in isolation but may not fit or not efficiently enough for our needs when evaluated in our overall "cultivating a people for God" objective. I encourage you to even create new materials based on your new insights because of our fellowship in this book. It will help us if we know in the beginning what we need to produce at the end when we approach to make a choice.

Harnessing the Power of Music

Now, let me say a few words about using music for Great Commission discipleship. Music is a very special channel for discipleship that is worth mentioning by itself. Words put to music have a magical power. Listeners and singers welcome beautiful melodies, and the music stay in their minds and the messages stay along in their hearts. On the other hand, truth well put into lyrics and music helps listeners memorize the truth. This is true for all age groups.

Church song leaders should choose music that fosters discipleship and not only for worship. I myself benefitted from such music discipleship. By the time I left my birthplace, Hong Kong, to study in Canada at age nineteen, I had learned over three hundred Christian songs, hymns, choruses, and choral pieces. I remembered the whole of Handel's *Messiah* when I was a teenager. I loved the composition and the interpretation by the Robert Shaw Chorale and Orchestra recorded in 1968. I sang it day and night and memorized God's work of salvation. When I sang these pieces, I came to appreciate His wisdom and power. Singing along with the vinyl records with Scriptural messages in the lyrics gave me an appreciation for God. Music made up some of the discipleship material I still carry. I learned more than four-hundred great Christian songs and their lyrics since then. Most of them are not the worship songs many churches would use on Sundays, but they are spiritually edifying compositions that have influenced my daily Christian walk with God.

After God showed me the Four Ships concept, I had a new perspective to interpret these rich resources in my head and heart. Worship, stewardship, fellowship, and discipleship cultivation were in many of these songs. There is also that balance among the four ships especially with older compositions. I still benefit so much from the spiritual experiences of the many songwriters and count them all as my teachers.

Get Excited and Get Into Action

Much has been said! Yet I cannot cover the topic of discipleship adequately in this short chapter. My objective is simply to relay the deep foundation of discipleship as much as I know. In conclusion, I like to invite you to envision churches and communities full of people who continuously advance in their spiritual walk and deepen their worship, stewardship, fellowship, and discipleship. What a joy to see and what an honor to be a part of this great showpiece for God and His ideal world.

In this chapter, we have retraced the roots of discipleship back to creation and into God's nature and God's heart—how God gave us the natural ability to be disciples and to make disciples. I have pointed out that in general, discipleship is the influence people have on each other. I have pointed out the need to intentionally tip the balance of all mutual influences toward God's will and bring people into a state of living well in His will—the Four Ships life. The vital signs of any successful discipleship program will exhibit true worship, stewardship, fellowship, and the resolution to multiply oneself in the will of God.

The Four Ships culture, the Four Ships disciples together, exhibits a powerful way to snowball discipleship. We may not need to change our programs in the churches but instead enliven existing programs by introducing the deep spiritual engagement with God's will and strategy. Every meeting opportunity, networking event, and even music can be making disciples. We should call everyone to cultivate a people for God in our discipleship programs. Along the way, we have painted a picture of the joy and happiness God and we would enjoy when true Four Ships discipleship happens.

Here, I have offered only a few key ideas to supplement what many able authors have written about. I hope this has injected new spirit and insights into your discipleship endeavor. May the Lord speak more directly to you about your needs in ministry! So come, join up in this process of discipleship, of cultivating a people for God. May God bless you when you say, "O God, I am willing!" I encourage you to evaluate, select, and apply all the good teaching materials based on the Four Ships framework and use your discipleship programs and activities to cultivate a people for God.

CHAPTER 11
Strength of the Four Ships Strategy

This chapter contains much of the original text published in my focus paper required for my doctorate studies at Fuller, and thus many references appear therein.

Summaries provide a framework that helps people grasp complex ideas. The Four Ships concept is my attempt to systematically present what God's comprehensive requirements are always for His people. It is meant to help us capture God's thoughts in the Commandments and the mission of getting His people back again for Himself. However, the Four Ships concept is more than a passing commentary; it provides a vision for those who want to express their love for God and is a simple spiritual framework they can live by daily, with confidence that they are practically pleasing God and spiritually walking with Him.

> Hear, O Israel: The LORD our God, the LORD is one. Love the LORD your God with all your heart and with all your soul and with all your strength. (Deuteronomy 6:4–5)

This passage helps us understand the summary and spirit of the Commandments given in the previous chapter. God Himself gave the commentary after He made the decree this second time. The Lord Jesus also helped us see the significance of this interpretation of God's requirement for His people when He replied to the Pharisees in Matthew 22:34.

Whereas the Ten Commandments and the mission in Exodus 19 are simple dry requirements, Deuteronomy and Jesus's summaries were about loving God and people with all our hearts. The Four Ships idea translates those requirements into a simple, integrated system that is readily doable in our daily agendas, and we can apply it to form and operate effective ministries. This integrated system helps us find balance among each of the ships in our spiritual walk and in church ministries. Simple frameworks also help people understand, remember, and propagate any worthwhile cause.

At first glance, the Four Ships approach to interpret the Commandments and the Great Commission seems to be just another way to say the same things many great people have already said about them. It is important to point out its specific strength so the merits and justification for using the Four Ships concept is established which are lacking in other approaches.

The four ships are a holistic, integrated, spiritual framework with firm and broad scriptural foundation that transcends time, place, and culture and bridges some of the schisms felt in the church ministries and religious life of many Christians. I will introduce how we can apply this spiritual framework even outside the Christian faith because it's rooted in God's design of humankind. I will draw your attention to how the four ships may give added strength to some existing movements among the churches globally.

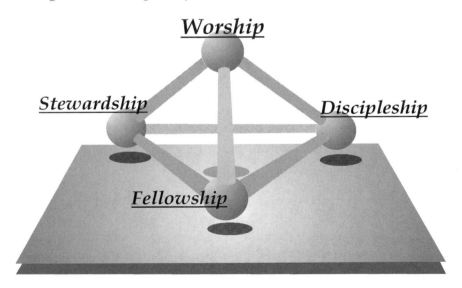

The Four Ships strategy is an agenda system based on the Great Commandments and the Great Commission. While I am given the picture of the Four Ships, I do believe that the Four Ships neither have the equal authority of Scriptures nor the Commandments and the commission themselves. If by God's grace, another agenda system is given to anyone to promote God's agenda, I will gladly submit to it. However, for now, let us continue to address God's desires using the Four Ships picture.

So, let us begin the journey.

Spiritual Relationship Essentials: Not Just Institutions and Programs

Like never, we have witnessed churches using new methods and trendy programs for growth and renewal. The effective use of need-based or interest-based social dynamics that resemble contemporary marketing approaches receives much attention. However, there is nothing that can replace the authentic practice of God-centered worship, Lord-honoring stewardship, heartwarming fellowship, and Great Commission–spirited discipleship. E. Lyle Schaller concurred that new programs and approaches to ministry were good, helpful, and even necessary to match the appetite of the seekers and Christians alike in today's culture characterized by competition, consumerism, and affluence.[37] Yet renewal efforts that focus on institutional and programmatic reform may miss the central issue of an individual's relationship with God. At least two examples in the Bible illustrate this assertion. One is in the Israelites' request for a king so they could resemble other nations: "You are old, and your sons do not walk in your ways; now appoint a king to lead us, such as all the other nations have" (1 Samuel 8:5). Another example is the people of the temple who sold sacrificial animals in the temple courts and dishonored the temple in the name of temple economy (Matthew 21:13). For years, many congregations were just like the chosen people in Malachi's times (Malachi 1:10). We considered ourselves Christ's churches and ran programs like a church but not necessarily in a manner God approved of. We faced the same prophetic words and risked having to close our doors for the last time just as many North American churches have had to do.[38]

Christians in many churches around the world are wandering in changing cultures and being pulled by secular influences and thus

---

[37] E. Lyle Schaller, The New Context for Ministry: Competing for the Charitable Dollar (Nashville: Abingdon, 2002), 14.
[38] Gibbs, ChurchNext, 10. Cole, Cultivating a Life for God, 11.

being discipled by the world. They try to stay politically correct. In some of the churches I have visited, ministries suffered decline while they maintained their traditions and followed popular church renewal movements. We must learn to stop and ask God, "Lord, which is the most effective approach to fulfill your plan in ministry among all these church renewal efforts?" I think the Lord Jesus will be happy that we asked, and His answer would probably still be: "Love the Lord your God with all your heart and with all your soul and with all your mind" (Matthew 22:37–40) and "Go and make disciples of all nations, baptizing them in the name of the Father and of the Son and of the Holy Spirit, and teaching them to obey everything I have commanded you" (Matthew 28:19–20).

The Ten Commandments and the entrusted mission are God's unchanging requirements. The fourfold emphasis on worship, stewardship, fellowship, and discipleship provides churches an agenda to implement ministries in line with God's heart. The Four Ships principles and values are God's desires for the way individuals should live and bring them closer to effective action plans. However, this concept does not force activities into context-dependent, mechanical programs like some other strategy concepts.

Unlike many program-oriented church growth and health proposals that emphasize institutional effectiveness, the Four Ships model emphasizes a holistic and balanced spiritual agenda (not a program) for fulfilling God's commandment and relational terms with Him. The four ships appear in every corner from Exodus to Revelation. They underlie minor and major themes stating and restating God's will and heart. We can read the Bible using the Four Ships framework and quickly understand God's heart for His people in the eternal timeframe. When we immerse ourselves in this journey of deepening, purifying, and engaging in our worship, stewardship, fellowship, and discipleship, we will be sure to bring God joy and blessings to people. This helps relate all we do to God's eternal plan and to our real-time relationship with Him. Such a spiritual path is well connected with our daily duties, productivity, and fun, and it adds joy, value, and effectiveness to all we do. When we are unwaveringly resolute in living such down-to-earth and up-to-heaven spiritual lives, we will certainly outflow with influence.

Few ministries can escape gradually increasing institutionalization over time. Time also contributes to a ministry's know-how and identifies which programs work and which do not. The experiences gained through growing pains help pave working paths and models for later leaders. Subsequent leadership and pastors who may not have gone or need to go through the original thinking and development exercise may trust in such no-brainer programs and strategies. Unfortunately, their motivation and mentality may become very different from those of the people who invented those strategies and programs. Later leaders would run the same programs and follow the programming pattern to the point they become institutionalized priorities. Thus, emphasis on program success and boasting institutional stability may become the foundation for many petrifying churches and parachurch organizations. This is not a new phenomenon and we can see it clearly in the last century. Many such successes in ministries are published in good spirit so others searching for working models may learn from their experiences. There is certainly a clear market for such materials globally, which snowballs and illustrates the phenomenon of the programming and institutionalization of ministries. However, we also find that those who sought these programs often cannot produce the success or results they hoped for. They repeatedly try out the programs and strategies and then switch models in time but sadly to no avail.

The Pharisees, Sadducees, and the Essences were the three major institutional religious sects at Jesus's time that had the same experience. These sects seemed good and necessary at the time, but over time, they became stiff traditions that lacked true spiritual salt and impact. They did not help their followers find God and His way as human traditions came about to cloud their theology. God had given them an opportunity like no other generation had - they were the ones allowed to ask the Lord Jesus that important question concerning the priority in their spiritual journeys. When Jesus answered the Pharisees' cross-questioning in Matthew 22:34–40 concerning which commandment was the greatest, His answer reflected very little of their institutional religious language. They were not the specific commandments the Pharisees were expecting. Jesus was neither in the Pharisees' nor the Sadducees' institutional or programmatic camps, and His vocabulary was foreign and surprising to them. The essence of the Lord Jesus's answer was that of the deep, loving relationship with God and humanity. That was in the spirit of the original Commandments.

Again, if it were not for the loving relationship initiated by God for us, we would have no reason for existence. God created humankind's physical, mental, and spiritual components so they would exist in a God-defined spiritual relationship, space and time. The environment designed by God demands that physical, spiritual, relational, and mental activities would align with His plan.

We received from God intelligence to make observations and experiment, and form habits so we would make wise decisions and choices. That was a masterpiece design by the Creator in His infinite wisdom and more importantly, in His free will. He chose and defined things that way. There is no authority that could rise to challenge Him or give Him better advice. God's love for us will always be the reason for our existence. The lost humanity will not find or redefine any valid new meaning through any institution or busyness in activities religious or otherwise. The futile quest for religious authenticity within the realm of fallen humanity met too many answers clouded by sin since Adam's fall. Jesus revealed the correct way: it is all about lives lived in all-out love for God and for our neighbors.

The fact that the Lord pointed to Deuteronomy 6 that summarized the earlier Commandments in Deuteronomy 5 is a strong implication for God's will for us to love Him and all humanity. Programmatic and institutional elements are not necessary evils; they are necessary channels and environments through and in which we express our spiritual essence. Yet, they should provide the time, space, and opportunities for us to live out our love for God and for others in real life as seen and heard in acts of worship, stewardship, fellowship, and discipleship.

The book *it* by Craig Groeschel describes a mystery, effects, and passions around the life-encompassing relationship between God and humanity. The Four Ships life helps to unveil that mystery. A life lived with God's will that centers on and balances the four ships is that original plan and blessing of God for us. When we live life like this, that is "*it*[39]" realized. I hope this sheds light for you when you read Groeschel's book. The Four Ships idea is a comprehensive spiritual sphere in which all human activities find meaning as defined by God. Balanced and proper practices in these areas fulfill God's will for us.

Contemporary Canadian culture—has been shaped by many influences. A tide of rebellious attitudes spread through the freedom movements in the 1960s in the United States and Canada.[40] Liberalism later flooded society through voters' beliefs and actions, and that affected government policies. The country embraced multiculturalism,

---

[39] Groeschel – the title of his book
[40] Kallen, *The Baby Boom*, 69–96.

and tolerance increased through the widened door for non-European immigrants. Immigrants and others cherished the shift and embraced cultural elements of their former homelands including religious beliefs without feeling out of place in their new country.[41] As the news media have tried to be politically correct, news about those groups as well as emphasis on gay rights, women's rights, workers' rights, and the rights of youth and individuals have received much attention and sympathy. Traditional Christian-based values and even the majority of the traditional core social values of the society were thus sidelined to accommodate the changing political correctness. Individualism and consumerism have overtaken the previous collective social values of the common good.[42] The Four Ships framework is a powerful anchor in God's will that stands against the aimless drift of the Christians in a chaotic society.

Renewed Spiritual Focus

The entertainment industry reduced its censorship of popular culture while tightening it for anything to do with traditional Christianity. Many sensual stimuli became acceptable. The tide swept across the society through the media. Christian leaders and pastors were not responding quickly enough in expressing their opinions, and the churches were not making disciples for Christ fast enough to slow down the cultural flood. Christians quickly became the minority and went on the defensive when the Canadian government promoted multiculturalism and equality.[43] The secular world seemed to have won the people away from churches and faith. People devoted themselves more to the pursuit of their Canadian Dream than to living lives of loving God and His kingdom.

When I was working as a programmer in the 1980s, politics and religion were two topics discouraged in office conversations. So-called political correctness took center stage[44] at the workplace. On the other hand, Canadian churchgoers expected the church to serve them instead

---

[41] Brian Seim, *Canada's New Harvest: Helping Churches Touch Newcomers,* 2nd ed. (Toronto: SIM Canada, 1997), Preface iv. Seim claims that 75 percent of the population of Toronto consists of immigrants and their children.

[42] Kallen, *The Baby Boom,* 78.

[43] Legislative acts that reflect Christian values such as the Lord's Day Act and the required recitation of the Lord's Prayer in schools were challenged and removed.

[44] Gibbs, *ChurchNext,* 22–23.

of them serving God[45] and thus drained more attention and energy from the church leaders, which slowed down the discipleship process further.

Meanwhile, churches struggled to maintain attendance. Different churches responded in different ways. Some soften their messages, renewing their music, changing the worship service, upgrading their buildings, and providing a greater variety of services to the community.[46] Many churches practiced some of these fads in the last few decades. In the process of stopping or slowing the decline, confusion in the church's ministry also grew because there was not an integrated concept to unite the many programs.

The devil used all these social movements to flood the minds and hearts of Christians and their pastors and to distract us from focusing on God's heart. The emphasis on the cultivation and practice of the four ships is an effort to call church ministries and individual Christians back to the original purpose of being God's people. It reaffirms the Commandments and the Great Commission using Four Ships terms to make sense for the contemporary minds. While not being program specific, the Four Ships concept emphasizes the inner being, spiritual discipline, and practical relationship with God, it stresses the inner motivation rather than the accomplishment of ministry tasks or personal pietism. The core values have strong biblical support and provide flexibility and support for contemporary creative programming.

Systematic Spirituality

The Four Ships spiritual framework integrates the Commandments and the Great Commission. It is rooted in God's creation and His redemptive and eternal purposes. On top of these, all parts of life can actually find their place in this system. We have absolute confidence that we may please God in this comprehensive and complete spiritual framework.

Relationship with God, not objectives

Most people enjoy the hope and the process of pursuing achievable goals. People are willing to commit energy and resources and even

---

[45] Ibid., 42–43.
[46] Ibid., 45.

acquire new abilities to attain those goals knowing the certain success. The pure psychological challenges of goals can often motivate Christians to engage in and commit to a spiritual journey and work toward certain spiritual disciplines. However, journeys motivated by seemingly spiritual goals may or may not have anything to do with Christians' relationship with God. People can spend hours in prayer for the sake of discipline but praying to no one except thin air. Even people who do not care to have a real relationship with God can do this. They may just want to feel good about their self-imposed spiritual discipline. Some people can be happy as long as they sound better or holier than others. On the ministry level, outward success such as getting a crowd, hosting big meetings, or growing church membership can become the main but impure motivation for church leaders and pastors.

Applying the Four Ships concept to cultivate a people for God is very different from some of those journeys described above. The Four Ships journey expresses a person's relationship with God in each "-ship". There is a growing deepening understanding of God's heart and His eternal will and plan. It is a matter of coming to know how God wants His crowning creation—humanity—to live and behave in His way out of love, respect, worship, and appreciation. It is a deepening response to God's supremacy, lordship, love and goodness. The God-fearing, loving thoughts drive the hearts of disciples who want to give God whatever He desires.

I am sure you would want to share my heart is this: I want God to have many many faithful, obedient, and loving worshippers in this generation. I want God to own many faithful servants who are serving Him and their generation. I want God to enjoy His children loving one another in His way. I want God to have many many more of the lost souls whom He created in His image saved. I want to help Christians live God's way. I love to see God having all of that. That is why I am in ministry even after retirement, and that can be why all Christians can live their love for God in rich, blessed lives according to His plan.

Deep Fulfillment

When Christians live for God by the His Commandments and commission in the Four Ships driven heart, they are in a constant, active, loving relationship with God. They will find deep, God-defined meaning in every step through ministry and through life. They will not need to continually hunt for the next goal to achieve. The sense of satisfaction and fulfillment can and should occur everywhere and at every moment the whole life long. God is honored, and humankind is blessed. Joy fills heaven and earth!

Continuity, Unity for all disciplines and people

Many of the discipleship schemes I encountered are divided into courses and levels that have varieties of objectives and even directions. The Four Ships Driven cultivation has only one direction and a single simple set of objectives for everyone from beginners to the most seasoned disciples. This also frees us from the spiritual caste culture in which holier-than-thou attitudes can fester while people focus on some spiritual ladder. It unites the journeys of those spiritually advanced Christians with the new believers. The Four Ships framework levels the playing field, and all can turn their eyes toward their common relationship with God, His work, honorable relationships, and the mission of discipleship. There are no waves of spiritual fashions and fads because we only adhere to God's unchanging will and instruction for His people. By God's grace, each Christian can participate in any activities or ministries and pursue the same essential and ultimate value of pleasing God. Instead of being divided and diversity all people feel and actually enter into a unity with a strong sense of fellowship.

Immediate Fruition

Unlike some spiritual disciplines that need time to develop life change or results, the Four Ships way instills immediate, life-changing truth that brings immediate spiritual fruit. The very moment a person decides to do God's will, God may harvest the fruit of dedication from heaven in and from that person's heart! The moment a Christian act in the heart for God in the worship, stewardship, fellowship, or discipleship spirit, another living sacrifice is readily given to God. The fruit of the four ships is internal and spiritual. It will soon produce visible effects and fleshed-out results in the community. I have witnessed that the effects of the fruit can spread to others quickly too. The community in which someone lives out any element of the four ships will be blessed immediately or in short order. There is no need for anyone to detach from family or hide away from his or her community to do Four Ships spiritual disciplines.

Complete, Comprehensive Biblical Foundation

The Four Ships systematic view helps us to see clearly the demands in the one and only comprehensive set of Commandments and Great Commission God gave for eternity. It calls ministry leadership and people back to the same basics systematically, not in a piecemeal fashion. It provides a single, simple, biblical focal point and channel for pastors, leaders, and congregants to relate to God as one people. It is encompassing that covers all teachings and requirements in the Bible concerning a person's walk with God. This is very powerful in bringing a simple unity and deep spirituality to churches.

Existing teaching material for faith seekers and spiritual masters should find a place in the Four Ships mindset and may still be used because of the completeness of the systematic framework. This is significantly different from what is currently available in the Christian education and discipleship marketplace. In many of those, beginner's courses and layers of advanced levels define the Christian journey. In the Four Ships framework, it defines only one direction and four simple disciplines. Everyone begins and ends there. Everyone knows that everyone else is just deepening and purifying each of the ships as each person encounters God in his or her relationship with Him. This helps reduce the pride of those who are advance in the journey and minimizes the stress and fear of those who are just starting to worship God in this way.

As the whole system stems from God's decree given for individuals and the people of God as a nation, the principles are valid for personal behavior and corporate ministerial actions alike. It points the way for combining individual spirituality and ministry, for the formation of communities and cultures, and for all humanity to actualize God's plan. This will help people to maintain the right motivation, the right course and make corrections as all watch out for their neighbors. It is God's will being done on earth as it is in heaven. Believers and church ministry leaders work for the same comprehensive purposes and values against the pressure of worldly culture to cultivate a people for God. The whole world can live according to God's way, engendering a God-centered, Godward[47] culture! Praise God for He is good!

---

[47] That is, toward God.

Supporting Ministry Structures in a Variety of Churches

The one and only God-given decree should be the broad foundation for all ministry structures and all forms of churches. Using the same foundation results in a consistent ministry in which people find that their spirituality matches perfectly with the demands and values of ministries. Church ministries can also be modularized by each of the four ships—the worship, discipleship, fellowship, and stewardship departments. A Four Ships ministry strategy unifies the church leadership team because each member and leader will speak and hear the same basic language and values in all ministries and planning committees. These common expressions of loving God and neighbors in and outside church bring the churches' ministries and Christians' lives into unity and harmony.

As this is the central will of God for humanity, it would naturally support, help purify, and give deeper meaning to existing church activities that are of God. Implementation of the Four Ships framework should not upset valid current programming. Only programs that are pointless in God's sight and empty of spiritual purpose or ineffective would be found in conflict with this purpose-driven framework. Any ministry structure or church form that finds issue with fitting in is in the wrong. If there is any program or activity church leaders found that does not connect well with these values, they should now have the courage and confidence to change or even terminate them.

Churches of all sizes can design programs or copy other church programs and build ministries that fulfill their call as long as they endeavor to practice the four ships. Health, effectiveness, and productivity of ministry should likewise be measured by the Four Ships concept and their contribution toward cultivating a people for God. The concept also provides a framework based on God's will for analyzing evaluating and identifying issues in church ministry as well as in personal spiritual journeys. This is tremendously helpful for pointing the way back to spiritual health and normality for both individuals and organizations.

Eddie Gibbs described some aspects of the changing North American church in *ChurchNext*. He suggested that church leaders had responded in various ways to their congregations' changing needs. While some leaders chart their own paths, some pragmatic church leaders use methods adopted from flourishing churches designed to advance church growth or stop the decline of their ministries.[48] In *The Purpose Driven Church*, Rick Warren introduced principles that had produced his church's growth. He believes there are dangers if people copy methods from more-successful churches, and he warns that those methods or programs may not always work because of differences in ministry context.[49] I observed this phenomenon of copying successful methods and programs when I worked in a bookstore. My customers would ask me, "Would this program work if my church were ... ?" I have encountered similar questions at church growth conferences that featured how-to programs.[50] Yet, when dealing with God's Commands and call to the mission, we must not use this kind of attitude. We are not qualified to ask for proof to see if God's way works or not. Our concern must not be how effective His way might be but how obedient and faithful we are in response to His decree.

Focusing on the disciplines of the four ships—worship, stewardship, fellowship, and discipleship—can positively affect churches of all sizes and diverse cultures. Every local church, large or small is a smaller unit of the universal church. Each shares the same collective calling as individual Christians. Every church can adjust its ministries, so they conform to the true fundamentals. Churches of any size can connect directly or indirectly with the values and spirit of the four ships. Ministry designs in churches of any size or culture may succeed if they are built on unchanging basic tenets. The ministry to promote God-centered worship (for the other "ships" too) can be for churches of any size—from small-group meetings at private homes to full-sanctuary events with thousands in attendance.

While the Four Ships fundamentals are not in and of themselves programs designed for producing church growth, they are the foundation on which such programs and methods can arise. Warren asserted that church ministries should be designed and evaluated around a stated purpose.[51] Whether simple or extravagant, church ministry structures can stay healthy when they seek to balance the elements of the four ships for the purpose of cultivating a people for God.

Under this scheme, worship ministry can include other kinds of

---

[48] Gibbs, *ChurchNext*, 232.
[49] Warren, The Purpose Driven Church, 27.
[50] I attended several of these programs hosted by the Willow Creek Association and the Purpose Driven Church.
[51] Warren, The Purpose Driven Church, 93–94.

activity beyond the usual Sunday service. Prayer groups and revival meetings that promote personal devotion and other spiritual disciplines are meaningful functions that the worship department can lead.

To promote proper stewardship, the church may create an organizational structure to handle finances, building and facility resources, and other units that support church ministries. Programs focusing on teaching spiritual gifts, personal resource management, and the cultivation of people's willingness to serve can be promoted under the stewardship ministry banner.

The fellowship ministry can organize activities to create healthy environments and promote Christ-centered functions in which people interact. These activities can include different kinds of small groups that bring people together. Sharing testimonies in small groups as well as in written form published in church media helps people get to know one another and build relationships. Christian education classes provide small-group environments in which people interact and learn from each other. The key for the success of a fellowship ministry is to constantly convey and promote the deeper God-pleasing relationships inside and outside of the church.

The discipleship ministry may include outreach and training phases. This ministry may train, organize, and promote outreach and evangelism teams that bring unbelievers to Jesus Christ. This ministry can also spearhead Christian education programs and promote Christlike discipleship through Sunday school, library, reading, and other small groups. The main purposes of Christian education and small-group ministries will be maturing disciples and multiplying and cultivating a people for God. This ministry concept can be implemented in any church yet stay within the framework of the four ships.

Useful for Analyzing Culture and Behavior

When God designed human, He meant for human to live respectful to Him, to be His representative to rule over His other creation, to be loving just like Himself, and be able to propagate physically and spiritually. When He gave the Ten Commandments and our call to mission in Exodus 19 the instructions are in harmony with that nature He designed. It is by this reason that the Four Ships concept will always works in any person's life. Some people may argue that it is difficult to quantify the God centeredness of a person's worship, the Lord honoring of a person's stewardship, the warmth of a person's fellowship, and how a person has witnessed publicly for the gospel. Yet the messages in both Testaments are full of such evaluation and even judgment concerning the performance of the chosen people (Haggai 1:5–8; Malachi 1:6–8, 11–14; 1 John 2:15–17; Matthew 5:5–7).[52] In the Malachi passage, the expressions and language used in a person's conversations over an extended time reveal a measure of the person's respect for God. Similarly, the Four Ships framework can be used to evaluate commitments and performance in our stewardship (1 Corinthians 4:6–7, 6:19–20; James 4:13–14), fellowship (John 2:9–11), and mission.

Similarly, we can identify the core values people hold by gauging their tone of voice, their vocabulary, and their focus in conversation in social relationships over time. This is true for individuals as well as groups and even nations whether God-chosen or not. We can identify the cultural values of individuals, a local church or any community. We can assess and evaluate the degree of conformity or alignment of a church to God's demand in scripture for worship, stewardship, fellowship, and discipleship. Any need for repentance and corrective actions may become clear (Haggai 1:5–8).

As for people and communities outside of the Christian Faith we can identify the god a person is serving by tracing that person's friendships and assimilation habits. Evangelically, we would hope that the god identified in such processes should be our God the Creator. However, the gods may also turn out to be those of health and wealth, the American (Canadian) Dream, specific church traditions, building programs, missions, their pastors, children, a hobby, or an unknown god. In reality, identifying the 'god' one serves may be the most crucial issue in the evaluative process as attested to in the chosen people's history.[53]

I believe the Four Ships approach can become a commonly accepted standard measurement of faith and ministry; and the theory that Christian leaders can use to assess a group's spiritual values and their relationship with God. The result can help individuals and churches return to the path God laid out for humanity.

---

[52] All our behaviors will be evaluated by the teachings of both Testaments. We can evaluate our performance in each of the four ships by comparing how we treat God and neighbors with how we treat other people and things.

[53] The stewardship, fellowship, and assimilation processes align naturally and logically with the object of worship. The Old Testament calls for repentance involved largely with the call to turn back to Jehovah. Once the proper person sits on the throne of one's life, the rest should naturally follow.

Ministry Health and Productivity Redefined

According to the Four Ships concept, Christians who practices the Four Ships model authentically and passionately would be healthy, productive, and most likely producing disciples. Likewise, churches that conform to the Four Ships fundamentals would likely grow and function productively in spiritual disciplines and multiplying disciples. The authentic practice of God-centered worship, Lord-honoring stewardship, heartwarming fellowship, and good news–spreading discipleship contributes naturally to and produces growth and health. The Four Ships concept is the platform on which popular church growth and health movements can identify their similarities and connections. This model provides a promising foundation to affirm and bridge the relationship of the church health and church growth proponents. It also supports and strengthens their foundations and confirms them as valid models to revitalize a church. The Four Ships concept connects personal, systematic spiritual practices and church ministry modularization that supports both on the same scriptural foundation. It bridges some of the schisms that Christians feel in the tensions among balancing the church, work, and social aspects of their lives.

Engender a Unique, God-Centered Culture

The conscious and deliberate practice of convictions in a pastor's life and the cultivation of the same in the followers' lives fit perfectly with *Merriam Webster* dictionary's definition of culture.

> 2: the act of developing the intellectual and moral faculties especially by education 3: expert care and training 4 a: enlightenment and excellence of taste acquired by intellectual and aesthetic training ... 5 a: the integrated pattern of human knowledge, belief, and behavior that depends upon the capacity for learning and transmitting knowledge to succeeding generations b: the customary beliefs, social forms, and material traits of a racial, religious, or social group; also: the characteristic features of everyday existence (as diversions or a way of life) shared by people in a place or time c: the set of shared attitudes, values,

goals, and practices that characterizes an institution or organization d: the set of values, conventions, or social practices associated with a particular field, activity, or societal characteristic.[54]

By the same definition, any culture can be eventually formed in time by the leader's modeling and teaching of any principles. The leader's beliefs, practices, style, or any other characteristic to his followers shape the culture of that community. As discussed earlier, the Four Ships model can put Christians and non-Christians on a similar conceptual plane and spiritual path. According to the concept, Christians and non-Christians share the same spiritual nature in behaving according to the God or gods they serve. They differ only in the identity and worthiness of the ultimate authority of the persons or things they worship. Who or what people worship is in effect the core reason for their daily choices. Non-Christians who serve money wholeheartedly have a money-worshipping life and fit into a money-ward four ships structured culture, while Christians who serve God wholeheartedly have Godward, Four Ships lives and are happy in Godward, Four Ships communities. Thus, pastors who authentically practice the Four Ships concept wholeheartedly and love God and their neighbors will start to spawn a Godward, Four Ships culture in their churches. When many people journey together in a uniform, Godward, Four Ships direction, then God-centered worship, Lord-honoring stewardship, heartwarming fellowship, and evangelism-oriented discipleship will become their cultural characteristics. We would have a Four Ships Driven Culture!

If we launch ourselves onto such a path, before we know it, a new culture will emerge among the congregations and communities that God welcomes and blesses. The original culture that God meant to see in humankind would spread powerfully. By living it and spreading it, we are cultivating a people for God. When churches become Four Ships congregations, the congregation would naturally participate in ministries. They would be happy as the outflow of their inner worshipful spiritual qualities and disciplines compel them for the action. Is this not renewal, revival, and growth? Institutional rules and programs would fall into their supportive roles to make way for the Lord's disciples to live out their ministries. The beauty and strength of these

---

[54] *Merriam Webster Dictionary*, 11th ed., s.v. "culture."

congregations would not be because of their institutional traditions or the good programs they copied from successful churches; it would be because of the essence of the spiritual qualities and relationships with God that He approves of and blesses.

The people in such Godward, Four Ships communities will certainly be filled with joy, hope and fulfillment. They will become energized agents for leading and cultivating other people to live according to these principles. Such a community will focus on objectives inspired by God's will rather than allowing habits or traditions to become their religion. Godward, Four Ships churches will also be free to design programs that fit individual needs that always fulfill God's will.

When this cultural reformation happens in more churches, it may gather momentum worldwide. Societies outside the church could understand the Four Ships model and allow people to reflect on their religious foundations. The worldwide, Godward, Four Ships culture will help to fulfill the Exodus 19 call effectively—God's people living in a holy way in obedience to Him and demonstrating His presence and blessings.

Strengthening the Foundations of Other Models

The Four Ships and Natural Church Development

Christian A. Schwarz's *Natural Church Development* (NCD) has a list similar to the elements in the Four Ships approach. Table 2 lists the eight essential qualities in the NCD concept reorganized and correlated with the Four Ships concept.

Passionate Spirituality	Worship
Inspiring Worship	Worship
Empowering Leadership	Stewardship
Gift-Oriented Ministry	Stewardship
Functional Structure	Stewardship
Holistic Small Groups	Fellowship and Discipleship
Loving Relationships	Fellowship
Need-Oriented Evangelism	Discipleship and Fellowship

Table 2. Eight essential qualities in the NCD concept correlated with the four ships

While the mathematical process of the NCD concept claims it as an 'exact' social science and is useful for quantifying quality for evaluation, the definition of health and success remains vague and runs the risk of mistaking social strength for spiritual vitality.[55] Even the list of elements in the NCD theory is based only on subjective incidental successes of the ministries surveyed and lacks authoritative affirmation from the scriptures.[56] This is where the merit of the Four Ships model lends its strength. Based on the similarities, the Four Ships principle validates the NCD list of essential qualities as being scriptural and on target based on the original commands and covenant between God and His chosen people.

Thus, even without the evaluative and remedial work of the NCD undertaken, the Four Ships holistic guidance should be applied prescriptively and preventively to develop people's spiritual lives based on the scriptures. With the backup of the Four Ships concept, there is added confidence in applying the NCD assessment process to track ministry performance and balance. Remedial programs may be formulated according to the NCD biotic principles to achieve or maintain church health.

Strengthening the Strategy, by Logan and Cole

The strategy Logan and Cole proposed in *Raising Leaders for the Harvest* is useful for multiplying disciples, Christian leaders, and churches. Their emphasis is on basic spiritual growth and numerical multiplication[57] of quality disciples to fulfill the Great Commission.

Logan's four-level leadership multiplication scheme highlights that leaders need all kinds of mutual influences through discipleship programs and coaching and mentoring processes where lives

---

[55] Gibbs, *ChurchNext,* 20. Schwarz, *Natural Church Development.* Schwarz's terms *quality* and *growing* as discussed in *Natural Church Development* have unclear definitions. These so-called qualities in the church survey are based on sociological elements such as opinions and common church language rather than on biblical, prescriptive guidance. This may reflect a statistic that is sociologically sound but may not conform to the scriptures.

[56] Schwarz, *Natural Church Development.* See note above.

[57] Logan and Cole, *Raising Leaders for the Harvest,* overview, 5–42. Logan listed and discussed an incarnation learning grid. The grid could have been used as the core spiritual foundation for their strategy, but as it is, this grid occupies a less significant role in their strategy. This grid contains all the Four Ships elements and can be regrouped according to Four Ships principles.

influence lives. However, neither Cole nor Logan discussed at length a relationship that actually exists between the life-transformation groups (LTGs) and the Ten Commandments. They claimed only that the LTG discipleship process was traceable to the Methodists[58] and was an accidental discovery.[59] On closer examination, it is easy to see that the LTG's mutual accountability query process has a direct link with scripture.

> These commandments that I give you today are to be upon your hearts. Impress them on your children. Talk about them when you sit at home and when you walk along the road, when you lie down and when you get up. Tie them as symbols on your hands and bind them on your foreheads. Write them on the doorframes of your houses and on your gates. (Deuteronomy 6:6–9)

Leaders who adhere dearly to God's commands and commission are cultivated by these instructions in their hearts. The Four Ships framework points out the value of implementing the instructions from Deuteronomy. Conversations around the questions in LTGs (see table 3) promote direct obedience to the Ten Commandments and the Great Commission. LTGs are crucial for carrying the Four Ships genetic principles (DNA) in the discipleship-multiplying process. The reading program and built-in, evangelism-oriented activities make LTGs a quality discipleship program that cultivates divine truth and nurtures relationships and apostolic missions (acronym: DNA)[60] according to Cole.

LTG Questions	Question Type
1. This week, have you been a testimony to the greatness of Jesus Christ with both your words and action?[61]	Great Commission

---

[58] Cole, *Cultivating a Life for God*, 60. On pages 55–62, Cole outlines his discovery of the LTG method of discipleship in a practical process rather than through a reflective process based on scriptures.

[59] Logan, *Raising Leaders for the Harvest*, 33. Logan described Cole's discovery as "accidental."

[60] Neil Cole, *Organic Church: Growing Faith Where Life Happens* (San Francisco: Jossey-Bass, 2005), 115.

[61] Cole, Cultivating a Life for God, 64.

LTG Questions	Question Type
2. This week, have you been exposed to sexually alluring materials or allowed your mind to entertain inappropriate thoughts about someone who is not your spouse?	8th Commandment: Dealing with adultery
3. Have you lacked any integrity in your financial dealings this week, or coveted something that does not belong to you?	7th and 10th Commandments: Dealing with stealing and covetousness
4. Have you been honoring, understanding, and generous in your important relationships this week?	5th Commandment: Dealing with honoring one's parents. The question is put in a way that helps extend the importance of relationships with parents to relationships within the home— spouse, siblings, and children. This is valuable, as not everyone lives with his or her parents.
5. Have you damaged another person by your words, either behind their back or face-to-face?	9th Commandment: Dealing with false witnesses or lies
6. 6. Have you given in to an addictive behavior this week? Explain.	This is a contemporary way of "serving another god," yielding to sensual temptations.
7. Have you secretly wished for another's misfortune so that you might excel?	10th Commandment: Dealing with some success that might have otherwise belonged to another person.

LTG Questions	Question Type
8. Did you finish your reading this week and hear from the Lord? What are you going to do about it?	First 4 Commandments: Dealing with worship and keeping the Sabbath to the Lord. Willingness to spend time reading the Bible and hearing God's voice is a fundamental spiritual discipline that keeps God at the forefront of our lives. The act of obedience is an integral part of worship.
9. Have you been completely honest with me?	The 9th Commandment: Dealing with honest testimony.

Table 3. LTG questions compared with the Ten Commandments and Great Commission

DNA is originally the acronym for deoxyribonucleic acid, the genetic code embedded in the cells of organisms. Thus, according to Cole, LTGs cultivate in the disciples another kind of DNA in its true genetic sense—the Four Ships core values of worship, stewardship, fellowship, and discipleship based on GC2. When this multifaceted genetic quality is passed on and multiplied through the LTG network and Logan's leadership farm system, a Four Ships culture can be achieved. Logan's leadership farm system and Cole's LTG discipleship program can be applied with confidence on top of the strong Four Ships foundation in order to fulfill GC2 and cultivate a people for God.

Strengthening the Purpose-Driven Concept

Another significant contribution to the improvement of the contemporary church health and church growth movement comes from Rick Warren's purpose-driven concept. His original work was studied and analyzed widely before he published *The Purpose Driven Church*. However, Warren claimed that the journey was a long series of experiments.[62] He stated that the purposes of fellowship, discipleship, worship, ministry, and evangelism were established based on Acts 2:42–47 and Matthew 22:37–40, 28:19–20.[63]

---

[62] Warren, Purpose Driven Church, 27.
[63] Ibid., 49, 102.

Warren's initial intention focused on making sense of church ministry. The idea of the purpose-driven life was only a subsequent development, obviously an expansion of the concept from the realm of church life toward a more holistic coverage. The key concept of being purpose driven stemmed from a description of a model with the *admirable result*: "And the Lord added to their number daily those who were being saved" (Acts 2:47); and not a prescriptive direction as found in Matthew 22:37-40 and 28:19-20,[64] Exodus 19-20, Deuteronomy 5-6, and Leviticus 19:18, 34. In the book of Acts, there are numerous locations where the number of disciples increased (Acts 4:4, 5:14, 8:9-13, 9:42; 17:12 to identify a few stories). Why was 2:41-47 elected above all the others?

However, Warren used these two Matthew passages later[65] in his conceptual development, but he did not fully leverage this passage and its Old Testament roots to give fundamental support for his stated purposes. It is certainly safer to base a strategy on prescriptive instructions as is the case with the Four Ships concept than on descriptive reports of incidental success. The Four Ships concept lends extra strength to Warren's strategy by supplying this prescriptive foundation.

On the one hand, I have exposed the weakness of the purpose-driven concept. On the other hand, I agree with and support the purpose-driven concept as both concepts hold similar values. These similarities are certainly appreciated. Table 4 demonstrates the comparison.[66]

Four Ships Key Concepts	Purpose-Driven Key Concepts
Worship (wider concept)	Worship
Stewardship (life-wide concept)	Ministry (more church-oriented)
Fellowship (wider concept)	Fellowship (narrower concept)
Discipleship (wide concept)	Evangelism, Discipleship

Table 4. The four ships and purpose-driven key concepts compared

The Four Ships concept is crucially more comprehensive than Warren's concept because right at the beginning and based on the

---

[64] Ibid., 102.
[65] Ibid.
[66] Warren, Purpose Driven Church, 103-7.

foundation of both Testaments, it integrates the core values of a holistic,[67] personal, spiritual cultivation and a corporate ministry orientation. It also leans more heavily on being in a personal relationship with God and ongoing spiritual cultivation rather than activities. The Four Ships framework for cultivating a people for God is a timeless, spelled-out, eternal purpose. As the purpose-driven ministry concept has seen God's blessings and enjoys approval among Christians around the world,[68] the Four Ships concept, based on prescriptive passages of scripture, may strengthen this already successful movement.

Bridging Discontinuities

The Four Ships concept strengthens church growth and health strategies and can help alleviate certain traditional issues Christians and ministries face. These include the discontinuity between personal and collective ministry agendas, the discontinuity in spiritual disciplines between seekers and new Christians and advanced or very spiritual Christians, and the discontinuity of ministry approaches between big and small churches.

In the last few decades, we have faced many challenges in bringing Christians together in a church to advance the common mission. Personal weaknesses and failures in God's people allowed the devil too opportunities to work against God's cause. Personal and corporate mission discontinuity existed even with Moses's ministry. God appointed Israel as a chosen nation to demonstrate His holiness and carry out priestly functions as God's treasured people distinct from other nations. Israel was to be a sign for the rest of the world of God's presence and grace. The chosen people and the rest of the world are invited to be in relationship with the creator God: "Now if you obey me fully and keep my covenant, then out of all nations you will be my treasured possession. Although the whole Earth is mine, you will be for me a kingdom of priests and a holy nation" (Exodus 19:5–6a).

The nation was to pursue the mission collectively, but God gave the Ten Commandments as action instructions to individuals. To honor God is a personal spiritual exercise. It is an individual's decision to create

---

[67] Involving all aspects of a person's life.

[68] Warren, *Purpose Driven Church*, back cover. This book has been circulated around the world in seventeen languages with more than five hundred thousand copies sold by 1995.

impressions that represent God or refrain from doing so. Merchants who are not idol worshippers must not profit from manufacturing images of God. The proper use of God's name, honoring one's parents, not stealing, not committing murder, and the other commandments require individual choices.

God seems to have intended the Commandments for individuals, but they are supported by national laws.[69] God gave us not only the Ten Commandments but also the detailed ceremonial requirements, civil laws, and the system of public sacrifices.[70] The tabernacle, sacrifices, ark of the covenant, choosing of priests and Levites, festivals, and all other ceremonies were national corporate rituals. They combined to form and support a culture that would guide God's chosen people as individuals so the collective people could achieve His mission.[71] The cultivation of worship, stewardship, and fellowship and the assimilation of Gentiles into the worshipping community form an agenda both for Israelite individuals and their nation.

The call for the New Testament church is similarly personal and collective as Christians work individually and together for God's mission (Matthew 22:37–40, 28:19–20; 1 Peter 2:8–9). We can translate Old Testament and New Testament agendas into contemporary terms, authentic God-centered worship, Lord-honoring stewardship, loving fellowship, and evangelism-oriented discipleship. Local churches and the worldwide church can thus establish ministries that help individual Christians flourish in their expression of the four ships: worship, stewardship, fellowship, and discipleship. The universal church can have a single Godward culture of individual and corporate obedience to Christ's mission using the Four Ships way of thinking.

As was the case with people in Old Testament times, many individual Christians live lives that deviate from God's instructions due to heretical influences[72]. This may be detected with the Four Ships assessment. As in biblical times, church ministries can drift off course as leaders follow unorthodox ways.[73] When leaders lead and individual Christians follow according to God's eternal instructions as seen in

---

[69] From Leviticus 1 on, religious law was given, and it merged into civil law in 24:17 on.

[70] Ibid.

[71] Ibid.

[72] Issues dealing with incorrect teachings are in 1 John, Romans, Hebrews, and Galatians.

[73] One example concerns the use of tongues in 1 Corinthians 12–14. Another is Peter's separation from the Gentiles in Galatians 2:11–14.

the Four Ships concept, together, they can fulfill God's mission as the new chosen people. Focusing on the four ships brings people together and resolves the tension between individuals and the mission of the postmodern church.

CHAPTER 12

The New Journey

My dentist Ron had involved in teaching an adult Sunday school class for a few years in the largest Chinese church in Canada, and he recently felt the need to explore more. As we shared our lunch this year before our dental business, he was excited to share his discontent with his sterile evangelical roots and how he found excitement among the charismatics. He told of the excitement of witnessing healing miracles.

During the conversation, he noticed I was not totally impressed. He said, "I know—the four ships, right? And you're going to debate with me."

I said, "Yeah I will, but please do finish."

"Is there something you found even more exciting?"

My answer was gentle. "Yeah, way more exciting. I have been so joyful since I found it, and I'm still trying to capture the fuller picture."

With that, he was ready, and I opened my mouth and continued to share.

"I do believe in miracle healing, but I'm surprised by the small game you're into. Quiet evangelicals and the charismatics lock into this small thing. Miracles, yes! Knowledge, theology, and exegetical teachings, yes—they're all important. Putting them together is like putting Niagara Falls, the Grand Canyon, the Great Wall of China, the Pyramids, and all the good and great sights of the earth together and calling them great—which they are—while failing to appreciate the mystery, glory, and beauty of the rest of the universe. The tug-of-war between Christian sects is but small things compared to what God has been doing in the grand existence in and beyond this universe."

Ron nodded and gave me permission to continue.

"God created the hardware of the universe, and He wanted humankind to be a part of His ongoing, dynamic, participative creation. As the beauty of a marriage is not in the good looks of the bride and groom at their wedding but in their ongoing working out of their good relationship, so it is with God's creation. The beauty of His creation includes the hardware and life-form systems but also much more. God created human beings in His image. Humankind has been such an important part of His desired relationship that their loss demanded His further sacrifice of His Only Son, who bears His full image, to save us, who share only a part of His image.

"God wants us to be a part of His ongoing project of creation in which an unfolding relationship will happen and its beauty will be demonstrated. Yes, I told you about the four ships. In a little while, when you clean my teeth, you'll be cooperating or co-creating God's creation so that the bigger world system may work healthily. Your stewardship is not something like giving some hard-earned money to the church but in real time while you faithfully use your skills on my teeth. God is pleased with your work. He is inviting you to offer your dental work to participate in His big project, yeah, that connects to the whole of the universe for the honor of His name and for His pleasure." Ron thought about it for a while, and then it was time for me to sit in the dental chair. Though I was asked to open my mouth, I could not speak anymore!

Ron had been a seeker on his spiritual path. He may have felt a renewed desire to search for deeper and truer answers. Each round of his search is a new start spurred by a sense of holy discontent.[74] You would not have read to this point if you had no holy discontent. Were you feeling inadequate in your theological stance? Was it a higher spiritual performance of some sort that made you desire to seek again?

Think about it—I have seen people seek advancement in their spiritual or religious performance so they can look as good as if not better than those who have impressed them. This may be by way of interpreting the Bible, giving a great lesson, delivering a memorable and moving sermon, or sharing an extremely wise comment. This may be in the form of a more powerful miracle, an exhibition of the filling of the Holy Spirit, an increasing number of hours spent in church activities, an increased number of roles in ministry, knowing or being the best-known preacher, going to an important conference, making

---

[74] I learned the term in Bill Hybels's Global Leadership Summit conference.

the most drastic spiritual transformation, and so on. However, we know that these spiritual abilities and blessings are but common water from the Samaritan well compared to the living water Jesus Christ offers us. It does not satisfy the deep thirst in our souls. Only when we find ourselves in God's will and having His approval do we find the satisfaction and fulfillment that can never be removed; because it is secured in God's book and heart. That alone is the true actualization of our humanity.

Ron called me the next evening exclaiming excitedly over the phone. As I was busy that evening, I requested that we end our conversation after some thirty minutes of joyful expression on both sides. The previous night, He had looked at the sky and saw only a few stars. Then his heart opened up as God spoke. Ron felt the invitation: to participate in His great work and become a part of the ongoing creation! Predictably, Ron could not fall asleep that night due to his excitement. He had a new start. He turned a new page in his life, and he will never be the same even after some thirty years as an active Christian.

Interpretation of Ron's Story

Ron's worship is no longer limited to church. His stewardship is beyond giving money; his relationship with people and his whole being changed from a self-interest-centered, self-oriented religious performer into a God-centered participant in God's creation. The Four Ships concept is the life-transforming truth that helped him to grow again on a new foundation, outlook, and philosophy for life, the universe, and God! His change was a deeper spiritual engagement in his relationship with God. He is more constantly mindful of the deep relational meaning in all he does.

Ron wanted to go on with that phone conversation, but I felt prompted to tell him he did not need me to give him all the insights. I told him that since he had opened his spiritual eyes, God would be able to use many people and things to speak to him about His will. Ron has caught a vision of the better place—a free space right before and under God's eyes, a place so free and vast, a place that it is not limited by denominational disputes or theological differences or the seemingly negative wording of the Commandments. A place where he can see so much goodness that there will be endless stories to share so people can draw closer to God! Now, Ron is more mindful of the meaningfulness of all things he does in life and thus enjoys a constant sense of actualization of a true disciple's life.

Ron taught Sunday school in his church and wondered what changes he had brought about in his students. In our relationship as friends and a dentist and a client, discipleship happened without planning or programming. There was no teacher or pastor in our relationship—just godly friends who shared out of our life experiences enriched with the truth concerning God's will. This process did not affect the existing programs of his church though it may make his Sunday school class looks less effective as he confessed. The potential is that without changing the programming of the Sunday school class, Ron is now in a position to bring life-transforming truth to his students and church so they can be closer to God's will.

My journey with Ron is no less than a process of cultivating one's life for God. We enjoyed the process with a great sense of fulfillment. A growing bond of friendship and spiritual fellowship develops in the process, which we are confident is pleasing to God. How did that happen? Well, I am just one God-loving, Four Ships life being active in living out what is commanded of me—to talk about God's commands and be concerned about His cause. I believe one by one or in classes or congregations, we can cultivate a people for God in time. May God grant us strength and blessings!

Visioning Changes

God had a will for His masterpiece—humankind. His will did not start with salvation but with a vision from before Adam came into being. The law given through Moses in the desert first spelled out His will so we would know what He desires at all times. We have been privileged to interpret it today in terms of the four ships. I hope this vision is like the green grass next door and creates a holy discontent in you so you will take action in your heart to pursue God's heart today. If you want to advance from where you are, where will you go? What direction will you take? Will it be better religious performance again? Will it be winning in the religious sophistication comparison game? Will it be a higher degree than your peers have? By God's grace, we are invited to come out of those small things into God's great cosmic project.

The many pursuits of spiritual excellence today have often not been very different from what the Pharisees and the religious leaders of Jesus's day sought. They look religious and are sophisticated, but they do not have much spiritual essence. This is so especially when the deep motivation was showing off self-achievement to others rather than pure devotion to God. The deceit of human hearts can turn all the truly godly, good things into detestable idol worship—where the biggest idol is the big ego in us. No wonder God allowed so many churches to close despite their desperate prayers for revival. Is this not the threat we are trying to fend off today in a big part of our church landscape? Clergy professionalism, scholastic achievement, religious pride, religious arrogance, complacency, and the like are but different forms of self-praise that rob God of His worship and lead to the deterioration of our stewardship, fellowship, and discipleship before Him, who called us.

But when we live out our worship, stewardship, fellowship, and discipleship according to God's original plan, we will know for sure that we are actualizing our humanity. Life itself becomes the opportunity to actualize God's creation in us by way of worship, stewardship, fellowship, and discipleship. We do all that for God's satisfaction and ours too—creating such a dynamic beauty for all to see and appreciate. How beautiful!

Changing the Measuring Tape

In the course of this book, we have unpacked the Commandments and the Great Commission and laid them out in the way of the four ships. This is done so that they can be readily understood and used for our spiritual navigation. Spiritual success needs to be measured by God's Commandments and Commission and the Four Ships is a good help for us to understand and remember the requirements.

I used to get poor marks in primary and secondary school because of a discrepancy between my schooling philosophy and the school system. I went to school for the sake of learning whatever I found interesting, whereas the school offered courses with a definite learning objective and a corresponding grading scheme. One ridiculous example occurred when I was in the first year of middle school. I was only thirteen and not yet interested in world history. I placed more importance on character integrity, especially honesty, than on mastery of historical details. I thought I should be marked for honesty! In the final examination, I wrote careless but honest answers "I do not know" all over the examination paper with no shame or guilt. To my surprise, I got a final grade of 4 percent for the course! I eventually learned that there are other objectives beyond morality in education, and these courses were meant to keep us focused on learning other subject matter. I knew then there was a specific marking scheme that was used to measure my performance. So I adopted the school's measuring scheme and studied accordingly and passed the subject the next year.

Many of us were led into spiritual darkness because for centuries too many leaders thought that God desires our sophistication in certain spiritual disciplines. Too many people had been buying into these wrong measuring tapes to evaluate meanings and success in Faith and life. This had created cultures that lead somewhere other than God's intended destination for us and Himself. Like my study of history in first year in my high school, we aimed for a wrong objective and moved along a wrong measuring tape. God has a definite objective for our lives. He will not examine our lives apart from what He has made and called us to be and do. Is it not a wise thing to dwell on the ever-consistent God-given Commandments and the Great Commission?

Reorganizing Church Ministries

I congratulate you if you have a spiritual discontent concerning your church ministry for producing more God desired results. The Four Ships way of cultivating a people for God may be the solution, a way out, a way toward the pasture to which God is beckoning you. Once you understand the measurement according to God's heart, you will have the courage to let go of everything that hinders your journey of walking with God. You will also have the creativity and determination to make changes including disposing of things that just serve habits rather than God in your ministry. You will be able to do the hard work and go through the difficult parts of the journey not relying on models but instead on faith and knowing you are doing God's will. Your ministries will not be just pursuing results but pursuing obedience to God's-command, though visible and quantified results will ensue. God will have a people His way—a Four Ships community and culture.

As we pursue what God wants, we should also organize our church ministries according to this new and comprehensive understanding of the Great Commandments and the Great Commission. It is then logical to have worship, stewardship, fellowship, and discipleship ministries in our local churches and denominations. I want to expand this concept in enough detail so you will not misunderstand my recommendation; but I will keep it brief enough so not to limit your creativity. Note also that none of the activities or programs should be exclusive functions within each ship's department. Programs and activities may consistently have one focus among the four ships, but other ships can occur conveniently and naturally. Much cooperation should exist to actualize unity in God as the departments work together. I think God will be pleased when we make that a high priority.

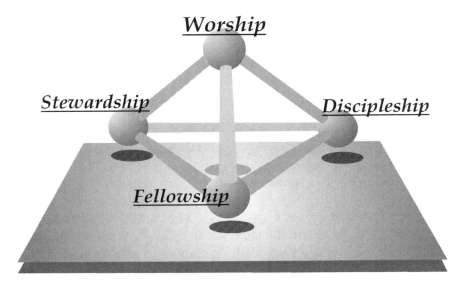

Worship Ministry

The worship ministry department should be responsible for *building a people of worship* for God in your church. This includes first but not exclusively Sunday worship gathering. The worship ministry cultivates the worship spirit in the congregation even beyond church gatherings. It should include programs to encourage personal devotion, meditation, and all forms of small groups that are devotional and worship (worship does not mean singing or music) in nature. The worship department should have team members who explore and study the meaning of worship. The measurement of the ministry's success is a reduction of self-seeking worship expressions while love for God and His honor is joyfully embraced. Stories of encounters with God and expressions of love for Him in people's conversations, in the Sunday worship, and in small group meetings should be the hallmark of a congregation that enjoys successful leadership in the worship department.

Different from many worship ministries, the worship ministry in a

Four Ships organization does not aim to have impressive Sunday music productions that are ends in themselves but rather to bring people and God together properly. Sunday or whatever day your church chooses to worship is but a renewal point of the weeklong worship beyond church gatherings. The head of this department must demonstrate a growing love and enthusiasm for God. He or she also does everything possible to make worshipping disciples.

Stewardship Ministry

Stewardship ministry may take all sorts of forms in different churches. Finance and facilities have been the two mainstays in this area in many traditional churches. It is not easy to change gears for most of those who are in the finance-only type of stewardship teams. A stewardship ministry in a Four Ships church will certainly include those areas like the old time.

In addition, the communications, information, leadership development, and functional organizational structures are important stewardship department issues; and should be managed in the church's stewardship group. Church boards, trustees, and sometimes deacons are typical members of the stewardship team. Stewardship also implies that Christians will apply their gifts and seek opportunities to get involved in all areas of ministry.

Matching gifts with tasks is an important part of being good stewards. Helping people involved in ongoing development should also fall under the care of the stewardship ministry. Churches may need to train or elect people to lead a Four Ships stewardship ministry. The reformed department leaders should demonstrate such a stewardship spirit that they influence or even deliberately train others how to be good and faithful servants of God in all areas of life. The financial management in the stewardship ministry not only encourages giving but also making faithful and efficient use of funds and facilities. They do not spend money according to the desires of the membership, or only concerned about financial viability of the church business operation but for God's purpose in the Four Ships spirit.

One or more branches in the stewardship department will be experts who train the congregation on how they may be good stewards in terms of personal finance, home economics, spiritual gifts, and personal resource management. When the stewardship team operates under the Four Ships model, there is a strong sense of spirituality even though the department still deals with many material matters. But when it is well reformed, there should be a reduced risk that the finance department will overrule the people cultivation ministries because of the power that comes from handling money.

Fellowship Ministry

The fellowship ministry in a Four Ships church will be responsible for building and promoting healthy Christian relationships among and beyond the congregation for God's pleasure. This will naturally bring blessings to the people. In my previous observations, too many fellowship ministries are social bound and lacking in the spiritual dimension. A Four Ships fellowship ministry should help people to build their fellow relationships within the framework of their relationship with God. The department does not have to organize all fellowship activities as there are already many occasions in the church where people interact. It only needs to promote how people should use a loving fellowshipping heart while they interact. These include any committees and Bible study, visitation and any occasion that people gather.

When the horizontal human-human relationship is enhanced by the vertical or spiritual God-human relationship, much strife will be stifled. The focus of the department is not on producing just social activities but also on using all kinds of activities to promote the spiritual-social loving relationships. The department would induce, monitor and maintain the spiritual dimension in people's relationship. A successful fellowship ministry will produce many happy people in the church, reduce relational issues and also help the church attractive and able to retain newcomers.

The Four Ships fellowship ministry encourages the construction of godly relationships and the reconciliation and repairing of broken relationships by God's grace. The department leaders should exemplify their discipline and teaching of grace and forgiveness. They should stay alert to help those who are having relational difficulties to attain reconciliation. The department seeks to please God in leading the congregation to become the hallmark of God's people, just as Jesus wished when He gave the new commandment of love in John 13:34. Imagine it! Does your church's fellowship program have a Four Ships spirit?

Discipleship Ministry

A Four Ships church should have a distinctive discipleship ministry. It includes outreach and evangelism ministries and can have cooperation with the other departments so people can be educated or cultivated toward maturity. Discipleship includes—Christian development as well as evangelism within the community and beyond which is traditionally called missions ministry. A balanced growth in worship, stewardship, fellowship, and discipleship is the rule for organizing systematic education such as Sunday schools and small groups.

Again, personal evangelism around the community and discipleship and evangelism beyond the church community are at the core of the discipleship department. The department is not about producing activities or programs but about implementing a process of leading people to become better and make new Four Ships disciples.

The existing Sunday school system, Bible study groups, Alpha, community outreach, and so on are all included in this department. The traditional Christian education ministry be an important part of this department's function though the scope is not as well defined now. So, you may always start the Four Ships reform within these existing ministries by simply adding the spiritual connection within the Four Ships mind-set and framework. The ultimate result is these departments should work together cultivating a people for God.

Watching Our Language

One important opportunity for the leaders of all ministries is in the meeting of ministry leaders on all levels. The secretary and the chair are very influential people in any church. The chairs of each large and small committee should take great care to conduct meetings with the mind-set of cultivating a people for God by the teams they lead. Conversations exchanged during committee and board meetings reflect the convictions each person brings to the table and the ministry. The chairs need to discern the logic and position each person takes and quickly and accurately discern the value system that backs up the opinion.

From the preparation and the agenda through the course of meetings and the minutes, we can help reform the ministries we lead. Wording and structure of the agenda should reflect the objective and direction of your team—cultivating a people for God using Four Ships values. The meeting should deliberately employ such language as the discussion generates and preserves the kind of culture conveyed in the language. The chairs should be helping the causes for those who speak in line with the agreed-upon Four Ships principles and not allow values inconsistent with those to creep in or take over. Secretaries should take great care to apply a Four Ships vocabulary and tone of words in these important documents such as the minutes and agendas. Chairmen and secretaries lead by their discerning listening and their words. We should never underestimate the great leadership opportunity that board and committee meetings afford us.

A Four Ships church needs no other ministry department. Anything else not mentioned above can and should be attached to one of the Four Ships departments. However, joint task forces can be formed when needed between the cooperating departments. If one department gets disproportionately large or drawing too much human or financial resources, that simply means the ministry is out of balance. We must trim oversized departments and strengthen weaker ones. This approach will help us clearly see what church ministries are working toward building the Four Ships concept and which ones are not contributing toward balanced growth. We must be brave to trim those that are just wasting resources so people can save precious time and energy and live fuller lives outside the church.

In time, a Four Ships church will demonstrate a culture in which people find God being honored and worshipped in spirit and truth. People should also find in your Four Ships church joyful faithfulness in everything the people do in church, at work, and at home. An open, receiving, fearless, and pure friendliness will be a sign to faith seekers and not-yet believers while the congregation will understand the love of God flowing freely among His beloved people. My friend, aren't you longing for such a community?

An atmosphere of welcome and a sense of readiness to lead people toward God is present in a Four Ships church. This is our dream church. No, this is Christ's specified church! The Four Ships church is efficient and effective saving people a lot of energy and time that they can use to outreach in their communities. There is abundant life outside of the existing church paradigm!

Beyond Church Gatherings: A Renewed Order for Earthly Things

Because the Four Ships nature was a design God used in forming individuals and human communities, it is natural that churches, communities, and relationships will work optimally when we follow God's track. What I have found in the past decades of practicing the Four Ships concept is that it provides a clear and workable guide for everything I do. I have used the insights in my personal spiritual walk, at play, at work, and in my relationships. I have used it in my pastoral ministry, in spiritual mentorship, and in relational counseling. I have also used it in church and business consultation, analysis, and troubleshooting, and it has even worked well in personal evangelism, premarital counseling. I am not surprised that it works because it is based on God's commands and is thus far superior to any other model. You too will be amazed and blessed if you take God's heart in this seriously. Ron did, Michael did, I did, and many others whose stories I have not included in this book.

You do have an abundant life outside of the church gatherings; not because church is a limited part of your life but because God designed you that way including life at home, at work and activities in the community. Yet His principles embedded in these four ships still follow you and help you live a fulfilled life in and outside church. God has His will for your work (mainly stewardship but the others too), your home (all four ships), at play (mainly stewardship and fellowship), and as a citizen (mainly stewardship and fellowship). As we live an effective life based on these four ships, we will attract a following and be able to cultivate a people for God. Soon, a cluster of Four Ships people among the churches will become a noticeable subculture, and that should have a great influence and become a visible phenomenon around the world. That is when God's name is greatly lifted up and honored as Malachi said (Malachi 1:5, 11, 14).

The Four Ships phenomena is constantly working in your life even if you do not know it or deny it because it is built into your life by God's creation. No one in the world can escape the dynamics. The difference is how conscious and well we purify and deepen each area before God. Follow the principles of the four ships. Keep much of what you are doing in your churches and at home but with a renewed mind and spirit according to the four ships. Pray a lot too to fend off the Devil's hindrances to your reformation. You will soon see yourself moving from where you are spiritually now and progressing on the path toward God's glory and your actualization as His creation. Please do call up your friends and tell them what you have experienced just as Ron did with me!

Yes, because the Four Ships principles have their origin in God's design of human beings, they are useful in every life setting. They should become the foundation of our educational systems, our governments (as much as the democratic system allows), our private lives, and our public life. They should become the foundation for building families and family counseling. They are useful at play and at work, in social relationships and in work relationships. They are applicable in business and business dealings, in friendships and family relationships. They are the foundation for managing the atmosphere, global resources, and the environment. By our practicing and building a God-centered, Four Ships culture, the world will be a very different place from what we see today. Apart from all the blessings, the happiest thing for me is that God is happy; and will say as He did at the end of the first six days of the universe, "This is *very* good."

Turn—Transforming Life toward Actualizing a Godward Culture

Pastor Edward shared a story during one of our weekly meetings. A woman in Taiwan was possessed by an evil spirit that spoke to her constantly of all the wrong things she had done. The voice, constantly about a meter behind and above her, would speak to her all day long wherever she went. Pastor Edward had been providing pastoral care to her, but he had to leave town for a few days. He entrusted the woman's care to a church elder that had heard about casting out demons by prayer but had never tried to do so himself. But then, he was stuck with a real-life case. Now that he had no choice, he decided to pray for this woman to cast out the demon.

As they worked up the faith and prayed for her, the demon promptly left. Of course, they were so happy, but the woman had a reaction to the situation. She thought, *That's it? It's gone? I'm not used to this. Maybe ...* At that split second of doubt, the sense of missing the old familiar friend within emerged, the demon returned, and everyone was stunned. The elder realized that the demon had returned; he had no choice but to pray again. That time, the woman knew what she had to do—to not doubt and not let that "miss my old friend" thought arise thus closing the door behind the departed demon.

Our thoughts are important in our spiritual transformation. If a positive thought to respond to God's Truth call comes, we have an opportunity to follow God's prompting and move forward. Suppressing the thought or faith on the Truth is the action of not opening our hearts to the Lord when He knocks. This would allow the Devil space to hinder God's work. Pray, pray, pray with faith in God!

Though I have talked so much about the four ships, this book is really not about the Four Ships culture but about pointing to a path that leads to God's heart—cultivating a people for God. Please, my friend, take the turn toward the Lord if He has spoken to you in spite of my imperfect words. This is no less than the action of faith. Eve's lack of faith in following God's command and decided to place her faith in the word of the snake led to the fall of humankind. You have this opportunity today to make the right choice. If the Four Ships concept spoke to you, turn to God in using it. If the four ships caused you to find a better approach to trust Him in all you do, by all means, follow that instead, and share with us that way.

May the Lord accept us as we trust and follow Him by obeying His prompting!

Our Journey Together through This Book

I have touched on the strategy for cultivating a people for God, but this book is not really about strategy, programming for the church, church growth, or personal spiritual renewal. I have not presented something like many other able pastors had for effective programs for church growth or renewal, nor did I focus on theology discussions concerning salvation, faith, orthodoxy, worship style, mission objectives, and many other things that improve churches. For such things, we have so many books written to a point of proliferation! I did not intend to write yet another one to add to your burden, but I felt the call to write this one long message. My objective was to call the church to renew its attention for the mission Christ; the Trinity has given the church to cultivate a people. Along with the mission, we have shone the spotlight on God's aching in His heart and His own instructions. These instructions are about how that objective could be achieved effectively - through cultivating the four ships in ourselves and spread that kind of life in God's household and beyond.

This book points out a clear direction for discipleship and pastoring God's people without pushing a specific program. It offers a new integrated frame of mind in personal spirituality, in church ministry, in the daily lives of disciples, and in God's people's social responsibilities. It does not limit but rather offers a new foundation that encourages you to be creative in designing whatever activities or programs in your ministry environment so you may join God in cultivating a people for Him. You can even use the concepts as I do to give effective advice to people to solve problems in church conflicts, for personal counseling, premarital counseling, marriage counseling, financial counseling, for young people's life planning and all other specific areas where people need advice. I listed the above areas because I have found Four Ships advice useful in all these areas personally and in helping people through their problems effectively over the years.

Apart from the life-transforming truth explored that charts out a new path for your spiritual walk with God, I hope our journey together has also opened a new window for exploring a new dimension in theology. The theology is no more about the traditional orthodoxy of the gospel, dispelling the heresies, fighting the Roman Catholic Church, drawing lines against liberalism or the charismatics, or sophistications in scriptural or historical studies. It is about a theology that takes much more consideration of God's heart before the creation account. It is about the image of God and His intention in creation. It is a theology of human's obligation to appreciate, worship and love God. I hope I stirred your heart for loving God in this book; I hope it will remind you of the deep and God-ordained original meaning of every part of our lives.

CONCLUSION

God has taken me on this journey on discipleship for over thirty years. It started in 1988 with my desire to seek His will and principles in church and ministry as well as for personal spiritual growth. I had not embraced too many marketed answers easily over the years. My journey involved several paradigm-shifts thanks to formal studies including two seminary degrees.

This book is not about a method or approach to solving the many problems individual Christians, churches, and the general population face today though the insights and principles are applicable for many such issues. I do not base my claim for the validity of the Four Ships principles on a program or model that worked in Jerusalem, California, or anywhere else at any time. I based my thesis on God's revealed will that He gave once and was repeated by the prophets and never revised. Our study through the course of this book is a journey taking us back to the heart of God before Creation.

The Four Ships principles may not be the only way to fully interpret God's will in creation, redemption, and the eternal meaning of human existence. Yet we should be sure any such theory and principle that base on the same prescriptive commandment foundation will be good too. This is because God's prescriptive direction presents a much stronger authority over any incidental successful model, such as in Acts 2:41–47.

Many writers have formulated answers to questions and concerns we have faced in the last two millennia. A simple internet search yielded a list of no fewer than a hundred issues people face today. Some of these issues concern the whole world while some are specifically Christian faith and church issues. Apart from the few issues that are on the order of natural disasters, the issues are all related to human activities. No wonder one responder to the internet discussion simply stated that the world's problem was "mankind" while another person echoed that with "Me, me, me."

Picking the right problem to solve is of utmost importance. Greasing the squeaky wheel without noting that the bearings inside have disintegrated will result in the wheel falling off. In dealing with the church and faith issues of decline—losing the next generation, leadership drought, spiritual dryness, the hedonic treadmill, loss of mission, and many others—without asking the correct key questions will similarly bring further problems. It will firstly waste our precious effort and secondly cause us to miss the opportunity to find a meaningful solution. In the process, we will lose our own ways and lead those who follow us astray. Third, it may cause further problems as those who followed the wrong solution will believe wrongly that the issue has been solved. Those who followed without thinking would become complacent and leave the real issue unattended. There may even be worse disasters than are mentioned here. But the most important thing is that we have a good answer when Christ holds us accountable for our lives and ministry influences.

I do not feel it is my calling to squeeze my voice into the lineup for attention in such popular topics like: church growth, turning declining churches around, spirituality, prayer, church governance, or any other smaller issues we face in discipleship and church ministry. My calling is to focus my energy so I can dedicate myself to following what God has given us in Exodus 19, 20 and Deuteronomy 6—to cultivate a people for God following His strategy. For that reason, I have to turn from following the popular trends.

This book is an interpretation of God's heart for what He wanted in the beginning and for eternity. It is also an invitation for you to consider the Commandments and the Great Commission as an integrated system that represents God's heart. By living and teaching them, we will have the best approach to fulfill the Great Commission, we will please God, and we will be blessed in the journey. It is about a call to prioritize properly among programs, implementation strategies, institutionalization, and clarity of the goals in God's heart (owning His people the way He wants). We have discovered a new path for transforming our minds and spirits so we can be living sacrifices for the Trinity God (Romans 12:1-3).

I hope you will find as I did the way of being God's people and how to do His work. I am confident that when you apply the four ships in a balanced way in your own life and ministry, you will find a fulfillment and freedom different from many of the theories or principles you found useful before. As much as your heart is seeking after God's will and plan, He is much readier than you are to reveal to you His mind and heart and bless you with the joy of knowing His will. I hope and pray the insights you capture in the Holy Spirit while reading this book will cause your life to be influential and effective in spreading a culture that is after God's heart.

I invite you to enter this new dialogue, give priority, love, and attention to God, and explore and pursue His mind and heart with a loving and submissive heart. I hope that new dialogues will take place in churches, seminaries, and wherever else people share this vision of cultivating a people for God with the same heart and mind for Him. I hope this fresh viewpoint and foundation will give you confidence in doing God's will and enter a path that pleases Him. Lastly, I hope at least that this book had at least stirred up your love for God.

Blessings to you as you faithfully and worshipfully carry out His will - of bringing a world to the Four Ships culture in which we can cultivate a people for Him.

May God be pleased and honored with our fellowship in this journey together. Glory to God in the highest, and blessings to all those who love Him. To God be all glory, amen!

APPENDIX A

My Early Discipleship Journey

During an internship term in my own church of about 450 people back in 1992, I was participating in the Master Life Discipleship program under the senior pastor. The small group met weekly to work through the manual and enjoyed the discussion and Bible exploration. The Master Life program taught six basic principles: spending time with the Master, living in the Word, praying in faith, fellowshipping with believers, witnessing to the world, and ministering to others. We can easily see teachings in worship, stewardship, fellowship, and discipleship in the objectives of the Master Life program. I do not know whether it was the program's lack of a solid foundation, my teacher's shortcomings, or my lack of understanding, but for some reason, I failed to connect the six principles taught in the twenty-four-week program with a unified scriptural base.

I am sure the materials we covered in the course were actually sound and good toward that end, but I found the sessions rushed as there was much to read through cognitively and the program led us by a very rigidly structured agenda. I did not have enough time to digest the material and connect spiritually to the teaching or the teacher. Before things had a chance to settle in my heart, we had moved on to another topic. That course experience gave me the impression that the ultimate intention of launching a discipleship program was to produce people who could deploy as church leaders for the sake of church growth in institutional strength and numbers.

The program seemed to focus on working through the material rather than learning from the leader's growing spiritual life or from his walk with God. If we had learned anything from the man, it was how he rushed us through the classes and the material. I felt very little if any spiritual life impact or transformation. I came through the program the same person I had been when I had gone into it. I did not wish to repeat what was done in leading others in such a program.

Needless to say, the short twenty-six weeks of training served more to instill material and program structure into my head than to cultivate my heart for God. The worst thing was that after our half-year course, we were told we were then ready to pass it on to the next generation of disciples. After we were commissioned, we never met again as a group or with the teacher. I could not even identify any sort of concrete idea about what spiritual growth was based on the course because the heady ideas and knowledge faded within six months.

Five years before I enrolled in that Master Life program, I had a much more positive experience. A master's class was offered to some of us in the same church, which had 350 people at the time. This program was a one-on-one, Paul-Timothy, gender-segregated, mentoring program. Much closer attention was given to the relationship between the disciple maker and the disciple. These training materials and methods were much simpler. They were geared toward a balanced cultivation of the person's spiritual disciple being and his ministry of disciple making. We went through scripture memorization, devotion, reading specified discipleship related books, and Bible study, as well as preparing our testimonies, taking notes during Sunday sermons and praying, all in a relatively loose way compared to the Master Life program. I must say that the first bunch of some twenty Timothys really grew well, though I could not say what the growth was, and the twenty or so Timothys-turned-Pauls were quite excited. A sense of movement was actually felt in the growing church. People were attracted to the congregation as they saw signs of a vibrant spirituality.

However, this program lacked the support of the senior pastor and the deacons. It died out after about three years with only a few Paul-Timothy pairs lingering. The program also lacked a long-term vision and extended meaning beyond a general sense of spiritual growth. It was a program with a beginning but without a clear, prescribed, ongoing path or deeper meaning. The program was never well developed.

The Paul-Timothy style discipleship program like the Master Life program lacks a connection to God in terms of relationship and His will. They focus more on the structure and specific personal spiritual disciplines possibly arbitrarily picked from a list of good things found in previous traditions. These programs eventually failed to satisfy the long-term discipleship needs of our church. The Master Life program had been ushered in five years later because of the shortcomings of the program before that. We hoped it would make a difference. Some five years after the Master Life's program was introduced, the church ceased to have a sustaining systematic discipleship program effort at all. We had tried ten years of discipleship and had little expectations for what discipleship programs could do for us.

The experience I had is not an isolated case. I had a meeting with a pastor friend at lunch the day I was writing this part of the book. He described almost an exact experience in his years of ministry. We agreed that failures in meaningful and sustained discipleship ministry happened not because of the lack of course material or programs generated by great strategies. The failures we witnessed happened because some of us had the wrong objective and thus a wrong approach in discipleship that led us to use the programs and course materials the wrong way. We found that the students would naturally learn not only the lessons but also from the life and modeling of the teachers. A classroom-based or small group–based discipleship course would yield only another classroom or small-group course, not disciples. I strongly agree with the following comment my seminary professor made during class one day: "You will take at least five years to unlearn what you have learned in seminary." I realized how true that was only a decade after I earned my seminary degree from that school.

Please do not misunderstand; I am not saying that discipleship programs are useless or that there is no need for prepared courses. What I mean is that we must realize the limitations of what programs and courses can do and thus exercise wisdom and apply sound principles as we choose programs to help accomplish our mission of making disciples. We must not be so tied and limited to what these programs prescribe.

Robert E. Coleman wrote about discipleship and presented us with sound principles that we can turn into activities and help us choose programs. As does Coleman's effort, the Four Ships concept lays a foundation of spiritual and discipleship specifications by which programs can be evaluated on the basis of their contribution to the cultivating a people for God. We must learn to distinguish the objectives.

1. Are we making disciples to save the church from decline?
2. Are we making disciples so we can have more people for our enjoyment in fellowship?

3. Are we making disciples to increase our personal influence in our churches? For church growth?
4. Are we making disciples to engage in a discipleship program?
5. Are we making disciples to serve the world—our generation?
6. Are we making disciples so more people will be blessed with the gospel and in their walks with God?
7. Are we making disciples for _____? (Fill in any other reason.)
8. Are we making disciples for obedience to Christ's Great Commission?
9. Are we making disciples in obedience to Christ and for God to have His people pleasing to Him as they walk with Him and do His will?

I recommend strongly that we should make disciples for cultivating a people for God.

BIBLIOGRAPHY

Anderson, Robert C. The Effective Pastor: A Practical Guide to the Ministry. Chicago: Moody Press, 1985.

Anisef, Paul, and Michael Lamphier, eds. *The World in a City*. Toronto: University of Toronto, 2003.

Anonymous, URL: Testimonials on page: https://www.experiencingworship.com/the-worship-study/ accessed on October 10, 2018.

Bandy, Thomas G. Kicking Habits: Welcome Relief for Addicted Churches. Nashville: Abingdon, 1997.

Barna, George. *The Turn-Around Churches*. Ventura, CA: Regal Books, 1993.

Bibby, Reginald Wayne. *There's Got to Be More: Connecting Churches and Canadians*. Winfield, BC: Wood Lake Books, 1995.

―――. Unknown Gods: The Ongoing Story of Religion in Canada. Toronto: Stoddart, 1993.

Biehl, Bobb. Mentoring: *Confidence in Finding a Mentor and Becoming One*. Nashville: Broadman and Holman, 1996.

Bowen, John, P. Evangelism for Normal People: Good News for Those Looking for a Fresh Approach. Minneapolis: Augsburg Fortress, 2002.

Clinton, J. Robert. *The Making of a Leader*. Colorado Springs: NavPress, 1988.

Cole, Neil. *Cultivating a Life for God: Life Transformation Groups*. Carol Stream, IL: ChurchSmart Resources, 1999.

―――. Organic Church: Growing Faith Where Life Happens. San Francisco: Jossey-Bass, 2005.

Coleman, Robert E. *The Master Plan of Evangelism*. 30th anniversary edition. Grand Rapids, MI: Fleming H. Revell, 1993.

Cordiero, Wayne. *Doing Church as a Team*. Ventura, CA: Regal Book, 2001.

Cosgrove, Charles, and Dennis Hatfield. *Church Conflict: The Hidden System behind the Fights*. Nashville: Abingdon, 1994.

Covey, Stephen R. *The 7 Habits of Highly Effective People*. New York: Simon and Schuster, 1989.

Crandall, Ron. Turn Around Strategies for the Small Church. Nashville: Abingdon, 1996.

Douglas, J. D., ed. *The New International Dictionary of the Christian Church*. Grand Rapids, MI: Zondervan, 1974.

Easum, Bill. *Unfreezing Moves*. Nashville: Abingdon, 2001.

Eims, Leroy. *The Lost Art of Disciple Making*. Grand Rapids, MI: Zondervan, 1978.

Eliade, Mircea, ed. *The Encyclopedia of Religion*. Vol. 11–12. New York: Macmillan, 1987.

Evans, Craig. *Mark 8:27–16:20. Word Biblical Commentary* 34B, ed. Bruce Metzger and Lynn Alan Losie. Nashville: Thomas Nelson, 2001.

Fabarez, Michael. *Preaching That Changes Lives*. Nashville: Thomas Nelson, 2002.

Foss, Michael. Power Surge: Six Marks of Discipleship for a Changing Church. Minneapolis: Fortress Press, 2000.

George, Carl. *Prepare Your Church for the Future*. Grand Rapids, MI: Fleming H. Revell, 1992.

Getz, Gene, *The Measure of a Church*, Glendale, CA; Regal Books, 1975.

Gibbs, Eddie. *ChurchNext: Quantum Changes in How We Do Ministry*. Downers Grove, IL: InterVarsity Press, 2000.

Gladwell, Malcolm. The Tipping Point: How Little Things Can Make a Big Difference. Boston: Little, Brown, 2002.

Groeschel, Craig. *it*. Grand Rapids, MI: Zondervan,2008.

Harris, Richard. *Unplanned Suburbs: Toronto's American Tragedy: 1900– 1950*. Baltimore: Johns Hopkins University Press, 1999.

Henrichsen, Walter A. *Disciples Are Made, Not Born*. Colorado Springs: Chariot Victor Books, 1974.

Hull, Bill. *The Disciple Making Pastor*. Grand Rapids, MI: Fleming H. Revell, 1988.

Horton, Michael Scott. The Law of Perfect Freedom: Relating to God and Others through the Ten Commandments. Chicago: Moody Press, 1993.

Huffman, John A. Liberating Limits: A Fresh Look at the Ten Commandments. Waco, TX: Word Books, 1980.

Hyde, Douglas. *Dedication and Leadership*. Notre Dame, IN: University of Notre Dame, 1983.

Kallen, Stuart A., ed. *The Baby Boom*. San Diego: Greenhaven Press, 2002.

Keener, Craig. *A Commentary on the Gospel of Matthew*. Grand Rapids, MI: Eerdmans, 1999.

Kotter, John P. *Leading Change*. Boston: Harvard Business School Press, 1996.

Kwan, Enoch. *Towards a 4-ships Driven Culture*, VDM Verlag, 2009.

Lageer, Eileen. *Common Bonds: The Story of the Evangelical Missionary Church of Canada*. Calgary, AB: Evangelical Missionary Church of Canada, 2004.

Lane, William. *Mark*. 2nd rev. ed. *The New International Commentary of the New Testament*. Edited by Gordon D. Fee. Grand Rapids, MI: Eerdmans, 1974.

Leggett, Donald A. Loving God and Disturbing Men: Preaching from the Prophets. Burlington, ON: Welch, 1990.

Levy, Sue-Ann, "'Toronto the Good' is in bad shape", The Toronto Sun, October 9, 2018. URL: https://torontosun.com/news/local-news/levy-toronto-the-good-is-in-bad-shape.

Logan, Robert E., and Neil Cole. *Raising Leaders for the Harvest*. Carol Stream, IL: ChurchSmart Resources, 1995.

Logan, Robert E., and Thomas Clegg. *Releasing Your Church's Potential*. Carol Stream, IL: ChurchSmart Resources, 1998.

Macchia, Steven. *Becoming a Healthy Church*. Grand Rapids, MI: Baker Book House, 1999.

Maxwell, John C. *Developing the Leaders around You*. Nashville: Thomas Nelson, 1995.

Maxwell, John C., and Jim Dornan. *Becoming a Person of Influence*. Nashville: Thomas Nelson, 1998.

Mayes, A. D. H. *Deuteronomy. The New Century Bible Commentary*. Edited by Ronald E. Clements and Matthew Black. London: Marshall, Morgan, and Scott, 1979.

Mead, Loren. The Once and Future Church: Reinventing the Congregation for a New Mission Frontier. Washington, DC: Alban Institute, 1991.

Minatrea, Milfred. Shaped by God's Heart: The Passion and Practices of Missional Churches. San Francisco: Jossey-Bass, 2004.

Nelson, C. Ellis. Love and the Law: The Place of the Ten Commandments in the Christian Faith Today. Richmond, VA: John Knox Press, 1963.

Nineham, D. E. *The Gospel of St. Mark.* 3rd rev. ed. *The Pelican Gospel Commentaries.* Edited by Adam Black and Charles Black. London: Penguin, 1968.

Packer, J. I. *Growing in Christ.* Wheaton, IL: Crossway, 2007.

Paterson, Tom. *Living the Life You Were Meant to Live.* Nashville: Thomas Nelson, 1998.

Posterski, Don, and Gary Nelson. Future Faith Churches: Reconnecting the Power of the Gospel for the 21st Century. Winfield, BC: Wood Lake, 1997.

Roxburgh, Alan J. Reaching a New Generation: Strategies for Tomorrow's Church. Downers Grove, IL: InterVarsity Press, 1993.

Schaller, E. Lyle. The New Context for Ministry: Competing for the Charitable Dollar. Nashville: Abingdon, 2002.

Schwarz, Christian A. *Natural Church Development: A Guide to Eight Essential Qualities of Healthy Churches.* Vancouver, BC: International Centre for Leadership Development and Evangelism, 1996.

Seamands, David A. God's Blueprint for Living: New Perspectives on the Ten Commandments. Wilmore, KY: Bristol Books, 1988.

Seim, Brian. Canada's New Harvest: Helping Churches Touch Newcomers. 2nd ed. Toronto: SIM Canada, 1999.

Senge, Peter. *The Fifth Discipline: Fieldbook.* New York: Doubleday, 1994.

Slaughter, Michael. Spiritual Entrepreneurs: 6 Principles for Risking Renewal. Nashville: Abingdon, 1995.

Spader, Dann, and Gary Mayes. *Growing a Healthy Church Complete with Study Guide.* Chicago: Moody Press, 1991.

Stott, John. *Decisive Issues Facing Christians Today.* Old Tappan, NJ: Fleming H. Revell, 1990.

Toler, Stan. The People Principle: Transforming Laypersons into Leaders. Kansas City, MO: Beacon Hill Press, 1997.

Van Gelder, Craig. The Essence of the Church: A Community Created by the Spirit. Grand Rapids, MI: Baker Books, 2000.

Warren, Rick. *The Purpose Driven Church.* Grand Rapids, MI: Zondervan, 1995.

Watson, David. *I believe in the Church.* London, UK: Hodder & Stoughton Ltd, 1978.